Dare To Be American

ZEB WEYRICK

ZAZ Creations
P.O. Box 384
New Prague, MN 56071

daretobeamerican.com

ISBN: 0692692851
ISBN-13: 978-0692692851

To Diane:
Thank you for the encouragement and inspiration you have constantly sown into my life. You allowed me to follow my own dreams and passions and support me at every turn.

To Scott:
Thanks for designing some amazing graphics and putting up with all the little changes I wanted.

To My Many Editors:
Thank you all for finding the endless number of mistakes, and providing great feedback. You guys brought this book to completion.

To My Readers:
Thank you for reading this book and taking responsibility for our country. Please write a review and share this book with your friends to get more involved in the renewing of America.

CONTENTS

INTRODUCTION

AMERICA NEEDS TRUE AMERICANS

America is fading and its fading fast, President Obama has almost doubled the national debt leaving it at $19 trillion, the Supreme Court has redefined marriage, and Obama has agreed to release $150 billion and virtually unrestricted access to nuclear technology to Iran. That's just the tip of the iceberg, but I think you get the point, recent administrations have been passing laws and making decisions Americans don't agree with and we the people are not stopping them.

It's been long enough. We've let government go too far, and now is our time to stand up and take responsibility for our country and our future. Next election, will you wake up, do some research, seek the truth, and vote for our future? Will you get off the couch, take some time away from your TV and be serious about your responsibility to vote?

The purpose of this book is to wake up a new generation of Americans and inspire them to take responsibility for the future of their country. I am a young entrepreneur who understands the state of our country and the responsibility I have to preserve its future. I've always had a dream of owning a large company that helps millions of people and I want to keep that opportunity alive. I want to make that dream a reality and help millions of others do the same. For that to happen there needs to be a land of dreams and opportunity, and America is that place.

I am part of a generation that has no idea what is

going on in our country and couldn't care less. We play video games and watch sitcoms and every now and then turn on the news for some, out of context, misleading soundbites. Some of us vote, but usually without doing any research or fact checking about the candidate. We hear about shootings and unconstitutional laws on social media but don't understand the significance of it. We are fed lies through the mainstream media and education system but don't know any better because we haven't read the Constitution for ourselves. We think it doesn't really matter when we vote because "no one would take away my freedom, and as long as I can watch *The Big Bang Theory* who really cares anyway."

This book is from one American to another, from me to you and I'm asking you to take action, to take responsibility, and to realize that liberal ideals and a growing government is killing the land of the free. This book is a wake-up call to a misled generation in faith that we will step up and take responsibility for our country. Do not believe the lies you are told at school or the misleading information on the news. Get your own information and analyze it against other sources and provable facts to determine its validity. Defend the truth, and the Constitution of the United States in front of your friends, your teachers, and your family.

Don't let the Land of the Free die on your watch, don't let your rights fade away without resistance, fight for morals, fight for values, fight for your freedom, Fight for America.

WILL YOU DARE?

"Posterity! You will never know how much it cost the present generation to preserve your freedom! I hope you will make a good use of it"
-John Adams

WHERE ARE WE?

America is on the cusp of death, its morals are fading, freedom feels more like chains, and high achievement is somehow being despised. Why is this happening? Why is America no longer American? Why is government pushing to take away the rights we are accustomed to, like our freedom of speech and our right to bear arms? This needs to end now! America needs to remember its roots and stick to them or it will be just like the rest of the over-regulated, bankrupt, government controlled countries in this world. (In case you're wondering, in this book "America" and "U.S." all refer to the good old U.S.A)

So what do we do about it? I dare YOU to read this book, learn how to be a True American and help me take back our country and restore it once again to a country that is for the people and by the people.

WHY DARE?

Being an American is a great honor, out of more than seven billion people you ended up in America, you are a part of the greatest nation on the planet, don't take that for granted. Yeah I'm bias but you should be too. If you live in America and don't think it's the greatest country in the world why do you live here? If you disagree with the American way, why stay? Why not move to a country that works the way you think it should, don't ruin America for the rest of us. Living in the greatest nation on earth doesn't come free or easy. In America you must take responsibility for yourself and your country, we seem to have forgotten that, which is one of the biggest reasons I wrote this book.

So to the point, why should you dare? Dare because if you don't there won't be a reason to dare, there won't be any honor left in being American, and there won't be a land of opportunity for your kids, and for their kids in the future.

Ever since America was born it has been the land of opportunity, a place of hopes and dreams for a better future. You should dare to preserve that and once again make this nation a place of achievement and opportunity. Dare to help the future generations, dare to help the poor and starving around the world, dare to make America the great nation of hope it once was.

BECOMING A TRUE AMERICAN

Being an American has great responsibilities and expectations. When you dare to be American you commit to taking on these responsibilities and upholding these expectations. First we need to know what the responsibilities and expectations are, so here we go:

#1 Most importantly you must take responsibility for yourself, your family and your future. It may be obvious but it isn't easy, taking full responsibility is a constant decision that can be easy to dismiss. Why does it matter so much?

If you aren't willing to take full responsibility for yourself, your family, and your future then you will be bogged down laying blame. When you don't make enough money you'll blame your employer or the economy. When your family doesn't get along or your kid starts doing drugs you'll blame your kids friends or the schools. When your future is looking down you'll blame your education or say you don't have enough time to make it better.

When you don't take responsibility for these things, you turn your environment into your enemy, and you sell yourself on the idea that your life is completely dependent on other people, all that does is leave you no way to change. It's a downward spiral that controls your life and starts to affect your future and the future of America.

#2 Be responsible for your country. You might be saying "How the heck am I supposed to do that, I'm not the president" Well taking responsibility for your country doesn't mean you have to solely make the decisions for the country's direction, no one in America should be doing that. America is a country that is, as Abraham Lincoln said "of the people, by the people, [and] for the people," we have all heard that before but currently we aren't acting like it's true.

This is where being responsible for your country comes in. If America is governed by the people, then we, the people, are responsible for our country, its current status, and where it is going. When our government started over-reaching so many years ago we, the people, should have stood up and said "Hold on, that's not how it's supposed to be."

We have been complacent in letting our government and the media control the people rather than taking responsibility for our country as we should. We have been electing bad officials and allowing a corrupt system of buyouts and favors for too long. An American stands up, takes responsibility, and stops over-reaching governments. After all, America was founded because of an overreaching, tyrannical King George III.

#3 Uphold the founding documents of America. Simply put, America was founded on the beliefs written in the Declaration of Independence, The Constitution, and The Bill of Rights. These documents provide a stable foundation and a basic law of the land for the republic of the U.S.A.

Since the creation of America our governmental system has been on the foundation of these documents. Sadly today our government has stopped obeying its limitations and the laws in these documents, it has been purposely misinterpreting and even completely ignoring them in some cases.

Did You Know:
The Library of Congress doesn't know how many federal laws there are today.

This is why we, the True Americans are needed and expected to know and uphold these documents as concrete law that limits our federal government to the small number of things it was meant to control.

#4 Live with a success mindset and fight for the American dream. America is founded with the idea that you can accomplish anything if you work hard enough. In doing so you provide for yourself and your family. You don't sit on welfare, or free government handouts, because doing so would be to fail and to give up.

Likewise when a fellow American needs help, it should be the community and the churches that help him succeed, not the government. If you rely on "free" handouts from the government for any extended amount of time you are not yet a True American, and you must adopt a success mindset. Look to the future, and make it a successful one. Don't give up and resort to dependence on the government at the expense of other's tax dollars.

Many Americans now believe that the American dream is dead. The American dream certainly isn't what it used to be but it is not dead. To achieve the American dream you must have a success mindset and be driven to achieve. Without a positive mindset you will never succeed and achieve the American dream.

Believe in and fight for the American dream. Do whatever it takes to keep this country free as a place where everyone can determine their own future. America was founded so that its citizens could be free to follow their own dreams and have the opportunities to do whatever they desire. Countless lives were laid down to create this land and yet we let our government stand in the way of this dream and even extinguish it further. We must oppose and stop the never ending stream of regulations and handouts. We must bring government back to the level it was supposed to be, to keep the American dream alive. Much power needs to go back to the states and the free market.

#5 Live with strong Values and Principles. America was made great by people who had strong values and stuck to them. These Americans were consistent in their actions because they made their decisions based on their values. They knew what they were fighting for, they knew what was right, and they stuck to those values and principles. Having strong values means that you don't waver, you make your decisions based on your unchanging values. When you do that your decisions are consistent. There are six values every American should hold, they are Responsibility, Equality, Courage, Independence, Authenticity, and Honor. Later chapters will dig deeper into these values and show their importance.

When we don't have congruent American values our decisions and our culture is like a failing roller coaster, you're here, you're there, you don't really know where you are or how long your ride will hold up. In general when you make decisions without values they contradict, they don't create an outcome congruent with what you intended and they create strife and complications. When Americans work together holding the same values and principles, decisions, direction, and destination are all congruent.

This is what made our country great, we had all the parts for a straight and efficient train. As we forgot our values that train turned into a rollercoaster. Now that we are losing them altogether the screws are coming loose and we see the ever growing divide and constantly elevating conflict and disagreement. Without congruent values sooner or later our rollercoaster will end in disaster.

Much more is to come, so stick with me and learn what you need to know to preserve this great nation.

Don't forget, We are the people, and We are the change, We are True Americans, and We Won't Back Down! Join me now and Pledge your Allegiance before we embark on this journey to a greater America.

I pledge allegiance, to the flag, of the United States of America, and to the republic for which it stands, One Nation, under God, indivisible, with Liberty and Justice for All.

AMERICAN ROOTS

"Liberty cannot be preserved without a general knowledge among the people"
-John Adams

WHERE AMERICA CAME FROM

America was born from action takers who were not satisfied with what they were told by their government and their church. They chose to think for themselves, get their own information and challenge the rest of their society. This led them on a gruesome path ultimately leading to the foundation of what is now the "Land of the Free."

I'm only going to get into the general story of these early Americans, but I encourage you to research this for yourself, learn the whole story, and get accustomed to gathering your own information.

Start Your Search:
Watch: *Monumental* by Kirk Cameron (More info at end of chapter)
Read: pilgrimhallmuseum.org

So back to the story of these very early Americans. It all began in England around the mid-1500s when the Bible was first available to the general public in English. As people started reading the Bible they learned about all of the lies the church of England had been teaching and sought a more Biblical church. These people opposed the teachings of the church of England and were known as the Puritans.

> **What Were the Lies:**
> **Read:** Martin Luther's 95 Theses,
> Luther points out that Biblically the Pope cannot sell forgiveness or control purgatory.

They stood for the Bibles literal teachings which opposed the tainted and added teachings of the Catholic Church and the Church of England. Now that these Christians had access to the Bible they could read it for themselves and no longer be bound by the agendas of their church and their government. At this time the king controlled the church and used it to further control the people, there was no separation between church and state. Because of this some groups of extreme Puritans broke away from the Church of England and started their own independent and illegal churches and were then known as Separatists.

One group of Separatists did not settle for their illegal underground church in England. They took a risk and gave up everything they had to find a place of freedom for their church and their children. This brought them to Holland where, at the time, they could be free of persecution for following the literal teachings of the Bible. After being discovered printing books critical of the church of England in Holland they risked everything once again as they went back to England in order to set off for America.

They first set out on two boats, the Mayflower, and the Speedwell. Soon after setting off, the Speedwell sprung a leak forcing them to go back once again to England. They decided that half of them would stay in England while the other half set out once again for America on the Mayflower. If you haven't guessed yet this group of Separatists is now known as the Pilgrims.

> **Did You Know:**
> Not all of the Pilgrims were Separatists.
> pilgrimhallmuseum.org/william_bradford.htm

It was situations like this that inspired America. It started from groups of oppressed Christians and daring adventurers looking forward, with optimism, to a free land for themselves and the upcoming generation. They gave it all to get to an uncharted land of opportunity for all who were willing to take the risk and persevere. The original Americans were born into a land prohibiting them from freely practicing their beliefs, but that didn't stop them, they took their circumstances and turned them into a brighter future which we now enjoy.

A TRUE AMERICANS FOUNDATION

The Pilgrims displayed some True American attributes we talked about in the first chapter, those attributes made their success possible. The original

American attributes they abundantly displayed are: Responsibility, a Success Mindset (Optimism), and Drive for the freedom that creates the American dream. The Pilgrims showed these qualities in abundance, and it shined through in a spirit of courage, faith, and persistence, which ultimately carried them through the hardships of reaching America.

Responsibility: Before the Pilgrims even got off the Mayflower they wrote a document called the Mayflower Compact. While this isn't a founding document of America it did start the bottom-up governing approach and showed their ability to be responsible for themselves and their future. They knew there would be immense stress and quarrelling in the months to come so they wrote a self-governing document to resolve those issues before they happened.

Success Mindset: The Pilgrims without a doubt had a success mindset. This was evident by their persistence, they kept fighting for a place of freedom. When they were found in Holland they didn't give up, they decided to journey across the Atlantic Ocean to a land that had only recently been discovered.

Journeying across the ocean at this time was no easy ride, especially on a cargo ship never meant for that type of voyage. The trip took sixty-six days, that's two months of unrelenting sea sickness, bitter wet cold, and living in a very small area with over a hundred other people. The "gun deck" is where the Pilgrims were for the duration of the journey. That deck's usable space was only a little bigger than a quarter the size of a basketball court, on top of that the ceiling was only five and a half feet tall. Don't forget some of that space was used for cargo. Once they landed at Plymouth they stayed in the mayflower for roughly another six months while they built their homes. During that first winter nearly half of pilgrims died.

Start Your Search:
Read: mayflowerhistory.com/cross-section/

They didn't start this journey expecting to die, even though that was a very real possibility, rather they believed that they would reach this new land and that they would be successful on their journey. They had faith and they acted on it with courage, and that's what a success mindset looks like. It would have been easy to conform to England and stay home, but they didn't, rather they forged the American dream of a better future, a future they controlled, where they were free and independent. Once they had this they didn't go back, not one of the colonists decided to return to England with the Mayflower.

Freedom of the American Dream: This is one of the most important aspects of a True American. This aspect is only possible if you have the previous qualities, without being responsible for yourself and having a success mindset you cannot effectively utilize the freedom of the American dream, because the American dream is completely reliant on the people pursuing it. The American dream doesn't rely on the government, if your American dream cannot survive without government subsidies or grants you need to ask yourself whether or not it is really the American dream. If your American dream relies on the tax dollars of someone else what are you really doing? If its valuable for the taxpayers that is fair, if it is not you are hindering their dream to achieve yours.

The Government was originally created to promote the American dream by defending our rights and freedoms to create equal opportunity. Sadly our government has grown and transformed into a government of millions of pages of laws and regulations limiting free market and hurting small business. It has also reached its hand into our personal lives with laws and programs such as nationalized school curriculum, national healthcare, and the heavy small business regulation.

The federal government was only intended to provide a fair playing field for all who play, it should not dictate what you do in your personal life, it should not stop you from expressing your beliefs and it should not dictate and administer advantages, bailouts, or subsidies. It should simply regulate crime and provide public utilities putting everyone on the same playing field under the same rules with the same rights.

Why is big government control bad for the American Dream? Put simply the bigger government gets the smaller the citizen gets, when the citizen is small their liberty is small. Big government hinders citizens liberty through laws, regulations, and control of whole industries. As the federal government grows and takes more control, such as through nationalized school curriculum, socialized healthcare, and increased regulations they start hindering your opportunity and ease of success. These actions completely change whole industries and crush the American dream for upcoming generations.

Why is it bad to give up liberty so government can control it? Well government is often very inefficient, schools tend to the lowest common denominator and don't reward individual achievement. Businesses (Current example, Healthcare) can't efficiently be run by bureaucrats that don't know how the industry works. Regulations make simple processes into expensive nightmares and usually don't improve the situation. Let's not forget big governments biggest downfall, when we no longer have liberty those in power can do with us whatever they please, it has happened many times in the past and it will again.

I will dive into what is wrong with our current government in a later chapter, but let this serve as an eye opener. Think about the recent events of these regulations in your life, have you noticed more paperwork and fees when banking or buying large ticket items? Do you have a small business struggling to keep up with all the regulations? Were you forced to pay for additional healthcare coverage that you do not want, or pay a penalty for not having it? Think about all the regulations you work around every day, do they make things better or worse? Do you feel more confident when you have to fill out twenty forms and sign a hundred million different things to invest money or buy a car? Do those extra signatures boost your confidence when purchasing such items?

TODAYS AMERICANS

We've seen the American attributes that were integral for the pilgrims success, but you might be wondering "what does a True American look like today?" From my perspective there are three types of Americans, there are True Americans, Fading Americans, and anti-Americans. (those who oppose America's heritage and ideology) The difference between these Americans stems from their end goal for America.

True Americans want to preserve and create an America that is free and thriving. They want to leave their kids with an America that is better than the one we have today, they want their kids to have more freedoms, more opportunities, and overall better circumstances. They recognize what contributed to the making of America and stand by it, defending the Constitution and the founding of our country. True Americans make responsible choices for themselves and their country even if it means personal sacrifice.

Fading Americans are more worried about the here and now. They make decisions that best serve them even if it means that tomorrow's America won't have as many opportunities or have the same freedoms. They don't uphold the Constitution, they buy into the lie that it is outdated and probably don't know what it actually says. They ultimately make selfish choices that hurt America in a seemingly indirect way, this includes those that can't be bothered to seek the truth before voting or don't vote at all.

Lastly we have the anti-Americans. These people often come off as meaning well but don't show it in their actions and results. They favor a socialistic form of government, and oppose Americas past by raving about all of the mistakes we have made and demonizing the great things we have done. This is an ever growing group becoming less tolerant of different ideas than their own. They often won't have a real conversation with you if you oppose their views, almost instantly resort to name calling and demining tactics. These people want much bigger government, they want a government that controls people from their speech to their spending. Anti-Americans oppose the Constitution, they call it flawed and claim it was written by flawed people, to them the Constitution goes against their agenda.

They ultimately oppose what America has always stood for and seek to change it into a country where there is an equality of result. They believe in a place where you don't build your success nor do you realize your failure, rather you share all with the society. They believe that it is in our best interest to all be equal in everything. While that may be well intended it results in all the high achievers leaving and the rest equal in mediocrity. Today's anti-Americans are found in associations such as the Social Justice Warriors, Feminists, and many Liberal Universities.

Below I have made a list of modern day choices and the decisions that the True and the Fading American would make. I have left out the anti-American because you should be able to determine who these people are. There is no middle here. You are either a True American working to preserve the American dream or you are a Fading American unknowingly letting America fade into the bankrupt and over regulated nation that anti-Americans seek. Thankfully you can always choose to take on your responsibility and become a True American. Whether you're a True, a Fading, or anti-American you can choose to help the country. America's future is completely dependent on its people, so we, the people, must do the right thing to keep our country alive and restore the idea and heritage of it

Decision to be made	Fading American	True American
How to get out of debt	File Bankruptcy	Sacrifice luxuries to pay off debt
Not treated fairly	File a law suit	Turn the other cheek and show compassion
Notice false teaching in public schools	Does nothing still sends kids to public school	Finds another option because the truth matters
See someone being abused	Look the other way it's not your business	Stand up for the victim
Sell a faulty product or service	Find a legal loophole	Take responsibility and make it right
Finding a dropped wallet	Finders Keepers	Find the owner
Government Benefits	Receive as many as possible	Does everything possible to stay independent

KICK START

- Watch *Monumental* by Kirk Cameron, this is a lively documentary on the origin of America and the journey of the Pilgrims.
- Read about the Pilgrim story at Pilgrimhallmuseum.org

IDEALS

"Democracy and socialism have nothing in common but one word, equality. But notice the difference: while democracy seeks equality in liberty, socialism seeks equality in restraint and servitude"
-Alexis de Tocqueville

Ideals, by definition, are; one's ideas of what is perfect, what a particular person sees as most suitable. So when you're talking about politics you get parties which are the groups of people that believe in the same ideals. This book is all about America so we'll only talk about parties and ideals as they apply to America as of today (2016). In America we currently have two main ideologies and two dominating parties associated with those ideologies.

Main Ideologies
- Conservative- Capitalist Ideals
- Liberal- Socialist Ideals

Main Parties
- Republicans
- Democrats

IDEOLOGIES EXPLAINED

Conservative Ideals focus on providing an equal playing field where everyone has the same rights, but it's up to them to make something out of the freedom they have been given. They think that government should be smaller, we should have free enterprise and that social issues should be solved outside of government.

Conservativism believes that a fetus has the potential of life and thus has rights, making abortion murder. They think that the government should not fund many research programs but rather that the private sector would do it more efficiently for their own motives. They oppose government controlled health care and support healthcare being truly part of the free market.

They believe that the government should do nothing more than make it easier for the people to help themselves, no favoring minorities or majorities. They think that long-term welfare is ineffective and rather believe in helping people get out of poverty through working for welfare and schooling. Conservatives think that the current school system is not working and schools need to be back in the hands of local governments.

Conservatives do not support amnesty for illegal aliens because it is unfair to all of the immigrants who went through the years of screening and thousands of dollars to get here. They believe in the rule of law, meaning illegal aliens are... Illegal. They also think that it is wrong to give out any kind of government benefit including schooling to an illegal alien. They do not belong here and it is unfair to those who do follow the law and pay taxes.

Conservatives believe that everyone has the right to display their religious affiliations even in government buildings. They also believe that Christianity was a big part of early America and what made it great. They find no problems with letting that heritage live on in our schools and at our government buildings.

Conservatives think that it is wrong to take someone's property even if you compensate them for it. They believe that when someone owns property it is their property and the government should not be able to take that from them forcefully.

Lastly Conservatives stand behind the second amendment as the right of the citizens to own and carry guns. They believe that the second amendment was written to protect the people from oppressive government as well as foreign intruders.

Capitalism is a system in which trade and industry are owned and controlled by private owners rather than by the state. Capitalism does not control and regulate your business, your success is purely dependent on what value you can bring to the market. It provides the same rules for everyone and does not discriminate based on where you start out in life. Under capitalism everyone has the option and opportunity to achieve great success.

Liberal Ideals focus on equal result and over all equality for all. They believe it is the government's duty to fix all the problems in the country and guarantee that no one is in need. They want bigger government and more regulations on enterprise and social issues.

Liberals believe that the woman has the right to choose to abort her child, and that it should be funded by the taxpayer. They think that healthcare should be government controlled and paid for through taxes.

Liberals believe that there is unequal opportunity in America due to race diversity and they think government should make up for that by giving minorities special handouts. Liberals think that public education is the most effective way to educate students and that all schooling should be paid for through taxes and federally regulated. They support amnesty for "undocumented immigrants" (illegal aliens) as well as believing that "undocumented immigrants" should have the same rights as U.S. citizens including their right to public schooling, healthcare, and welfare benefits.

Liberals think religion should not be associated with government in any way even as far as not letting individuals express their religion in government buildings. They think that government should have the right to all property and that the owner has no rights to his property as long as he is compensated for it. They think that the second amendment reserves the right to bear arms for the government only and that the death penalty is too harsh a punishment regardless of the crime.

For the most part Liberals want bigger government. They believe that the only way to create a fair society is by having a large government to regulate, grant, deny, and redistribute per the wish of the majority vote. When it is all put together it becomes a democratic-socialist style of government and economy.

> ### What is Democratic-Socialism:
> Socialism with a democratic government; the community as a whole owns and controls the means of production, capital, land, property, etc. and controls it through democratic vote.

Socialism is a system in which the community as a whole owns and regulates production, distribution, and exchange. Socialism hates competition and wants to keep everyone more or less at an equal level of power. Socialism is a system where the government heavily regulates the economy to redistribute resources and wealth among the population. It tries to create a more equal outcome from the economy by providing an unequal playing field. Socialism is a system in which you are limited as to how much you can achieve because you are regulated and required to help and fund those who are not driven to achieve. It takes away the motivation to achieve. Socialism is not a fair playing field but rather a teeter totter. (I'll talk about this more in a later chapter, don't worry this is just the boring chapter - they get more exciting.)

REPUBLICANS

Republicans are the party of the conservatives, they want to reduce the size of government and create a truly equal playing field for all. Republicans are usually entrepreneurial people, they are business owners of all sizes and they highly value the free market and what it does to create the American dream. Republicans believe that America did not become the greatest nation on earth because of the redistribution of wealth or high taxes. They wholly believe that the strong entrepreneurial spirit and get it done attitude of America is what made it great.

Republicans want to preserve the aspects of America that made it great and continue to improve upon those aspects so that America does not cease to be great. Republicans like to look to what has worked in the past to put in place new ideas based on facts that work and logical improvements for a better future.

That being said there are some modern republicans that do not truly stand for these principles, they are republicans in name only (rino). They claim to be conservative but go right along with the liberal's agenda. These republicans are usually career politicians. (meaning they have been a politician their whole career) Career politicians usually cater to the voters and popularity ultimately landing them more so on the liberal (left) side.

DEMOCRATS

Democrats are the liberals, they want more government regulation, less competition, and more "equality." Democrats think that America needs to improve, they think that capitalism is unfair and ruining America. Democrats want to look to the rest of the world to see how countries are being run and make America more like them. They think that America was successful because it has many resources and "stole" what it doesn't have from others. They usually value diversity, equality, and academia.

Democrats want to take away certain American

freedoms in the name of equality. They want to model after the rest of the world instead of stand out. They like to look to new ideas that have no logical standing and call them ideas that "haven't yet worked" (such as our welfare system.) They think that more government regulation and intervention will fix moral and economic problems. Many modern democrats don't value the entrepreneurial spirit, they think that it is unfair for one person to work very hard and achieve so much when another is achieving so little.

THE FIGHT FOR AMERICA

There is a major battle in America between the liberals and the conservatives. As you saw they are very different in their views on how things should be run and they are losing sight of what they are really fighting for. We are all Americans and we should all be working toward making America the greatest country on earth.

That can only happen if both sides can get along and fight for a common goal. Liberals will have to give up on turning America into a democratic-socialist country like many of the other countries in the world. Conservatives will have to work with liberals to find a better solution for lifting people out of poverty and lowering the wage gap.

One thing is for sure, every American that loves what America stands for, and used to be, needs to work together to make this country great again. Everyone who lives in America and wants it to be like another country on earth, with a socialist system of government and less free market should just move to one of those countries, there are plenty to choose from.

We need to accept that America is the only county on earth with capitalist roots. In less than one hundred and fifty years after declaring independence America was the biggest economy on the planet, and I guarantee you that is because of a **Free Market** and a strong **Entrepreneurial Spirit.** If America is going to be great once again, it needs to stick to those roots. People do not flock to America because it has an increasingly regulated economy, if that were the case they would also be trying to flock to Canada, Denmark, Finland and so on. They aren't. We received four times more immigrants than Canada in 2012 and that is only looking at the legal immigrants, if we look at illegal immigrants we house more than twenty times more. (Albeit illegals are mostly our fault)

The United States of America will not be better if it's like the rest of the world, specifically Europe. If that were the case then we would not have been the greatest country on earth. Let's remember Europe had a big advantage, it is much older than America, it just had one big hindrance, large controlling government systems. If Europe knew a better way to run a country America would not be getting worse as we adopt more and more European policies.

True Americans know that America needs to get back to its roots. We need to fight for the American dream and the freedom of the Capitalist system. It made us the world's biggest economy in just a couple hundred years, and it is proving to work once again in China, India and many other emerging countries.

KICK START

- Start putting more value on true freedom
- Look at the people in history that held each ideal and examine the results of their leadership
- Watch some videos by PragerU on YouTube, PragerU is a informational channel that breaks down big political issues into simple digestible videos.

THE FOUNDING

DOCUMENTS

*"The people are the rightful masters of both Congresses,
and courts, not to overthrow the Constitution, but to
overthrow the men who pervert it"*
- Abraham Lincoln

America was founded on three main documents, the
Declaration of Independence, the United States
Constitution, and the Bill of Rights. You have heard
of them, probably even read them once or twice in
school but do you really know what they say? I bet
you don't, so this chapter will serve as kind of a boost
to get you interested in them and teach you a little bit
about who wrote them, why they were written, and
how they were intended to be used. If you would like
to read them right now I have put them in the back of
this book along with some additional web resources
for understanding them.

I encourage you to read these documents and be
familiar with them because they are the foundation
for our government. If we as citizens don't know our
rights; than government can easily take them away

with laws and actions that are beyond the power they are given in the Constitution. What's worse is; we won't know we have lost our rights till it is too late. As Lincoln said in the quote from one of his 1859 campaign speeches it is the peoples job to defend the constitution from those who pervert it.

DECLARATION OF INDEPENDENCE

Who: Thomas Jefferson, he was born to a very prominent family of the planter elite in Virginia. Jefferson had a thirst for knowledge and started studying Latin and Greek at the age of nine. When he attended the college of William and Mary he bonded far better with the professors than with his peers. He later went on to study law and did so for twice as long as the average lawyer. When he was done he was one of the most learned lawyers in America.

He was first elected to the house of Burgesses in 1768, and in 1774 he wrote his first major work, "A Summary View of the Rights of British America." Following that work he had established his reputation as a strong proponent of the American revolution. A year later we was elected to the Continental Congress and placed on a committee to draft the Declaration of Independence.

The committee was made up of five people including Benjamin Franklin, and John Adams, who in turn tasked Thomas Jefferson with drafting the Declaration of Independence.

Did You Know:
Thomas Jefferson was just thirty three years old when he wrote the Declaration of Independence.

Jefferson worked on the first draft over the course of seventeen days, he used some material from his previous work in Virginia but did not draw directly from outside sources. He first had it revised by John Adams and Benjamin Franklin before it was approved by the full Declaration committee. It was then presented to the continental congress, where a fifth was changed, most notably the part against slavery. It was then passed by congress and sent to print on July 4th.

Why: The Declaration of Independence, is exactly what it says it is, its main purpose was to break ties and declare independence from the King of England. But it did more than just break ties with Great Britain, it expressed the idea of a new form of government where the people were the focus. It acknowledges rights given to us by God that are everlasting and unalienable. It respects the citizens, their rights, and their power.

The Declaration of Independence started the idea of a government that doesn't try to oppress and control its people like every other government at the time did. The Declaration of Independence is what sets America apart from the rest of the world, it recognizes the natural rights God created us with and gives the power of government to the governed. The Declaration of Independence states that the purpose of government is to defend the rights of the people and give them individual liberty. Our government was formed by citizens to secure their God given rights, Life, Liberty, and the Pursuit of Happiness, from enemies of those rights both foreign and abroad.

Intent of use: As previously stated the original focus was to break ties with Great Britain and accuse the king of his injustice on the Colonies. Thankfully Jefferson and the rest of our founding fathers thought much broader than that. Although that is what the document focuses on, it transcends time and protects the people of America still today, that is, if we know and defend it. The Declaration of Independence tells us that a government should get its power from the people and when the government becomes destructive and harmful to its people it is the right, and duty of the people to alter or abolish it. They must then build a new government on the foundation of the principal that government is for the people and for the protection of the their rights.

THE CONSTITUTION

Who: The Constitution was written at the Constitutional convention by collaboration of fifty-five delegates. Representatives from each state (except Rhode Island) joined at this convention to collaborate and amend the existing Articles of Confederation. It didn't take long for them to realize that this would not be enough; a new constitution would be needed. Our government was always meant to represent the people and this is how that was accomplished. James Madison as well as the other Virginia delegates were early to the convention so they wrote what would become the frame work of the Constitution. This frame work was known as the Virginia Plan and it provided many of the ideas for the constitution; the biggest being the separation of powers. The

Constitutional Convention took place from May 25th till September 17th 1787, and during this time the constitution was written. Madison is often considered the father of the Constitution due to the framework he laid out before the convention as well as his work in the Federalist papers which contributed a great deal to the interpretation and adoption of the Constitution.

Why: The Constitution was written to create stronger centralized government that could better defend against rash political movements and foreign threats that could harm the country. The Constitution replaces the Articles of Confederation, which was quickly created to form a weak government holding the states together during the Revolutionary War. Our Constitution serves as a foundation for our government and provides a process to protect our rights and our freedom.

Intent of use: The Constitution is meant to give specific power to our federal government and provide a framework for its operation. It disperses the power into a system of checks and balances and gives each branch a different power. It separates the federal government into three branches, the Legislative branch, the Executive branch, and the Judicial branch, each carrying out different functions of government. This keeps the ultimate power in the hands of the governed removing the dangers of a handful of government leaders doing whatever they please.

There is a lot to understand about the Constitution and how it works, so I encourage you to do some research on your own, check out the sources I provide at the end of this chapter and find some of your own so you can get a good grasp on how the constitution is intended to work.

THE BILL OF RIGHTS

Who: James Madison was also the leading author of the Bill of Rights. He was the son of a successful planter in Virginia and the oldest of twelve siblings seven of which lived to adulthood. Madison was sent to boarding school at the age of eleven and later went to what is now known as Princeton University. While at Princeton he studied Latin, Greek, Philosophy, and Science. Madison served in the Virginia militia as a colonel for a short while but soon put his better talents of writing to work at the Virginia convention in 1776. Around that time he met Thomas Jefferson and they became lifelong friends. Madison was also appointed to the committee in charge of writing Virginia's Constitution, while on that committee he worked with George Mason who's work on the Virginia Declaration of Rights would influence Madison when writing the Bill of Rights.

He served in many different areas and worked on many things in Virginia before writing the Bill of Rights. Most notably he championed the separation of church and state to strengthen Virginia's Statute of Religious Freedom.

Madison later went on to be the secretary of state under Thomas Jefferson and the fourth president of the United States.

Why: The Bill of Rights consists of the first ten amendments to the Constitution and puts specific limitations on the government adding one more level of protection for the citizens. Like George Mason, many of the states that did not agree with the Constitution believed that it needed a Bill or Rights to fully protect the people, and so it was written.

Intent of use: The Bill of Rights is intended to protect the rights of the people making it clear what the government should never have control over. It lists certain rights that every citizen should have regardless of what the government thinks. This provides a very effective way of keeping the power in the hands of the people as well as giving them a legal foundation to stand on should they need to defend themselves against an over-reaching government.

WHY DO WE HAVE THESE DOCUMENTS?

Our founding fathers wrote these documents to protect our rights and our freedoms. These documents lay out a form of government specifically designed to protect our freedom and create a fair playing field of individual liberty for our lives. These documents were intended to stop the overreaching government we have now.

Our government should not be making hundreds of new laws and regulations every month or even every year, and it should not be trying to take away or change the rights that are given to us in the Bill of Rights. Our government has crossed the Constitutional line, it has surpassed the power given to it from these documents and now it is our duty to enforce these documents and reform.

Know your rights, and know what power is given

to the government. Study these documents and understand them so our current government, school systems, or mainstream news outlets can't mislead you into giving up any more of your freedom. A perfect example of how they are trying to mislead you is their strong opposition and broken reasoning behind limiting the second amendment. All of these institutions are pushing to extremely limit or take away our second amendment and if you don't know what the second amendment actually says you could fall for their shenanigans. It is time to stand against our increasingly unconstitutional government and fight for freedom.

KICKSTART

1. Read the founding documents and think about what they mean as you read them. (You can find them at the end of this book)
2. Learn more about the Declaration of Independence by going to Heritage.org typing Declaration of Independence into the search bar and clicking on the first result after the yellow box.
3. Understand the Constitution by going to heritage.org/constitution you can click on any part you don't understand or want to know more about.
4. Take the free Constitution class from Hillsdale College just type "Hillsdale College Constitution 101" into google and click on the first result.
5. Encourage your friends to read and understand the Founding Documents as well.

WHY AMERICA IS

IMPORTANT

"Liberty, when it begins to take root,
is a plant of rapid growth"
-George Washington

You may have been convinced otherwise but America is important to many people all around the world, often more so than to those that live here. For most of America's existence it has been a light, a hope to the rest of the world that there is a place where your dreams can come true and where you are free to pursue them. America has been a country founded on Christian values in love and compassion, helping in every way we can, not just doing so out of selfish desires.

America has been an example of putting aside our personal beliefs to transcend all cultures and religions, banding together with the idea of liberty and hard work for a better tomorrow. America has led the way in revolutionizing how the world thinks about how people should be treated. America is the greatest advocate for true morality and justice, but all of that is fading pretty fast now. The world needs America and it needs America to remain a moral and free nation because if it isn't the world will lose its hope.

Before you all go crazy about the bad things the U.S. has done in the past remember to put it in context. Any time hundreds of thousands of people from different culture groups are put together there will be some that do bad things and those few will convince others to follow in their ways. That is nothing new, it has been happening since the beginning of time, and it always will. America took that downfall and created a new way, a way that limits the power of the few as well as the power of the mob and gives all an equal say. At least that's how it is supposed to be, however, today we see that failing as our integrity fails.

The comparing game is a dangerous game to play but if you compare the bad things America has done, to the bad things the rest of the modernized world was doing at the same time you'll find an interesting result. The bad things we did the rest of the modernized world was doing as well. That does not excuse us or make it any better, but it does show that we were not the unique evil of history the Left often blames us for. What is unique about America is that it so quickly turned from those ways to a new and moral way of life.

Every country on the planet at some point took land from a different culture group, to a certain degree we did to. The U.S. was formed when we gained our independence from England, from there we bought already concurred land from the French in the Louisiana purchase which included land from Montana to Louisiana. As we moved west our federal government, led by President Andrew Jackson, broke treaties made with the Indians and championed the Indian removal act of 1830 resulting in the Trail of Tears.

Later, the independent republic of Texas joined the U.S in 1845 and a year later a border dispute between America and Mexico started the Mexican-American war. After America won, the Treaty of Guadalupe Hidalgo was signed in which the border was settled, Mexico recognized Texas as part of the U.S., and the territory north of the Rio Grande was purchased for $15 Million plus forgiven debt Mexico owed. It is worth noting that President James Polk, instigated the Mexican war which was seen by those on the Conservative side to be unconstitutional.

When it comes to slavery the U.S. did bad things, I'm not disputing that, what I am disputing is that America is worse than the other countries at the time. For instance Europe had been trading slaves for more than 300 years, that's longer than the U.S. has even been a country to this day.

Portugal was the first into the transatlantic slave trade in the late 1400s, the first recorded British involvement was in 1562, Spain got involved in the early 1500s, and other countries such as France, Norway, Denmark and the Netherlands also played big roles. It took more than 200 years before Britain, the first to abolish the slave trade did so. In contrast after gaining independence America participated in slavery for 89 years before the tension between the slave owners (South) and the abolitionists (North) was so great that there was a war to abolish it. More than that before our country was even independent from Great Britain we were pushing to end slavery. A clear example of that is Jefferson's opposition to slavery in the original rough draft of the Declaration of Independence.

There are still an estimated 21 million people in modern slavery around the world, it's not the same as we had in our past but it is still forced labor or forced sex. We should be working on stopping modern slavery, creating a better future for those still in slavery around the world rather than having sensational but useless "Black Lives Matter" and "Feminist" protests here. These groups of people may have started out useful with a good cause but at this point they are back tracking the progress that has been made. The actions they take and the reasons they use just fan the flame and make them look in the wrong.

No matter what you believe the past is the past, it is time to stop playing the blame game and build a better future. We need to stop dwelling on what our country did wrong in the past and start recognizing that it has done far more good and we must continue upon that good, learning from the past but not letting it bog us down.

WHY AMERICA IS GOOD FOR YOU

If you've lived in America your whole life you probably haven't realized just how lucky you really are. America is an amazing place in almost every aspect. I'm not going to focus on why America is good for you, but rather I'm going to help you realize it yourself. I've been to five different countries in my life and every time I leave, the list of things I'm grateful for grows dramatically.

When I was seventeen I visited some missionary friends in Kenya and while I was there I noticed how important community responsibility is.

From my experience in Kenya everything is kind of thrown together, they have a beautiful landscape and some amazing animals but day after day they slowly ruin it. Most make do with what they have and don't think about what they will need in the future. They are constantly cutting down trees to use as fire wood and neglecting to plant more. They don't maintain their land so although they have trees for fire now they will soon run out leaving many of them helpless. They lack the emphasis on responsibility for the future that we strongly encourage in America.

Kenya also lacks the responsibility needed to create a clean community. They do not handle their waste responsibly. There is random trash littered all along their roads and it is rarely if ever picked up. In America when we see some trash on the ground we usually pick it up and dispose of it somehow but in Kenya this community responsibility is missing. Granted they do not have the same ease of access to proper waste management we have here, but overall the community lacks the responsibility for their waste that we enjoy here.

When I visited Guatemala I realized just how important it is to have a community of honest people. I visited an orphanage in Guatemala and while I was there the missions leader for the orphanage told us that we could not go outside the walls of the orphanage especially not alone. He said if you go out there and turn right you will be raped and if you turn left you will be murdered. There was a major lack of honesty and integrity in the community as well as the law enforcement.

In America we have a community of people who are honest and responsible. Our community stands up to criminals and puts importance on good morals. We also have law enforcement that for the most part is honest and works for the people. This results in a safe atmosphere opening up many opportunities that would be very hard to realize in Guatemala.

When I visited Northern Ireland (U.K.) I noticed a general lack of optimism. For most of them it was just the daily grind, they didn't dream much of what they could achieve in the future and what they could improve in their country. In America far more people look to a brighter future and they work hard to achieve it. Most Americans will look at what can be improved not just what has to be fixed. The spirit of optimism is part of what helps us work hard and achieve so much. Without it we would be bogged down in the daily grind and never find the time or take the opportunity to improve.

Did You Know:
Americans are more than twice as likely to say they are having a good day than Europeans

Read: pewresearch.org/having-a-typical-day-in-2014-youre-not-alone/

After traveling to several different countries I realize just how important mindset is. In Kenya for the most part their mindset lacks thought of the future and of community responsibility. In Guatemala the community lacks the mindset of honesty and integrity. Lastly in the U.K. they lack the mindset of optimism. The American mindset has taken the best, most productive ways of thinking from different cultures all around the world and purged most of the hindering thought processes. This is what makes America special, we understand the importance of our mindset.

WHY AMERICA IS IMPORTANT TO THE WORLD

By now you probably think I'm some self-serving jerk because I think America is extremely important to the world. You're probably thinking I should humble myself and lay off the strong doses of straight America. Give me a second, let me explain why America is important to the world.

The first thing that makes America important is our Liberty. America was built on the idea of freedom and individual choice and for its whole existence America has been a place people look to in hope of escaping their oppressive governments. America has been that city on a hill, that light in the darkness for those who want to make a better life for themselves and their families. It has been a place of dreams to build the life you've always dreamed of.

America became that place because we recognize the rights of the people and created a government designed to protect Rights rather than grant Privileges. The idea of individual rights changed the world and creates inspiration for many. It shows people that government is not responsible for you, but rather you are responsible.

In America we take that for granted, we forget that many countries don't allow the freedoms we have here, we forget that other countries have governments that reserve all power and grant certain privileges rather than protecting inherent rights. That is all we should need to fuel the fight against our ever increasing government and its overreaching control. We need to not only protect our rights but also the concept of individual rights.

Even more than just being a light of hope and encouragement America helps the starving and oppressed all over the world, in fact we care so much about helping that we go in debt for them. Our government is so adamant on helping everyone else in the world that it is destroying us at home. Take our foreign aid for example, in 2013 we spent around $40 Billion dollars aiding 194 countries, that same year we went $642 billion further in debt, we give away money we don't have. It's good to help other countries but if we sacrifice our economy to help them we will end up hurting far more.

We've seen what our government gives on our behalf now let's take a look at how Americans help voluntarily. Feed My Starving Children, is a Christian non-profit based in Minnesota. In 2015 FMSC fed around 628,000 children every day, that equates to a little over 229 million meals. This is possible by having over 898,000 volunteers packing meals to send to the 70 countries they currently serve. FMSC is just one relatively small example of hundreds of thousands of organizations in America helping those in need around the world. America is full of people willing to donate their time and money to help those in need and that is one more reason why America is important.

Today the U.S. makes up just 4.4% of the world's

population but we produce nearly a fourth of the world's GDP and in 2012 we did about 17% of the worlds manufacturing. This is possible because America created a place that draws in inventors from all around the world and provides the freedom and incentive to innovate. We invented mass production which originally made the car, and now basically everything else cheap enough for the general public to afford. We invented the telegraph, the cell phone, the TV, the airplane, and the home computer. You could almost say we invented most of modern life. Socialism doesn't do that, Capitalism does that.

We were the first country to fully implement a truly free market and today many countries have adopted some form of a capitalist economy. To date it is estimated to have lifted around a billion people out of poverty. China adopted a free market system in the late 70s and early 80s and since then more than 680 million people have been lifted out of poverty in China alone.

America is also important to the world from a moral stand point. We are the moral compass in a mislead world, at least we used to be. We are a moral compass because we have integrity, freedom, and equal rights. Our citizens are morally responsible enough that when given that freedom they don't abuse it, without moral citizens freedom cannot survive.

We fight for a land where it truly is a fair playing field for all who live in it. After many years other countries have started to follow our lead but none value freedom and rights like we do. We are not just a city on a hill but also an inspiration for change in other countries.

AMERICAN IDEA

America isn't just a country, it isn't an ethnicity, it is an idea. I hope you have heard that before but even if you have, do you really know what it is and how to describe it? If you don't you're in luck because it is so simple that you cannot forget it, yes I mean that literally. You can't forget it because the American idea is printed on every American coin. I learned this from Dennis Prager, he calls it the "American Trinity." These three parts are In God We Trust, Liberty, and E Pluribus Unum (From Many One.)

The American Idea combines faith, freedom, and equality. (Not the modern-day idea of equality however) These three parts of the American idea create basic principles such as the Rule of Law, Unalienable rights, and a limited Government. These ideas put the power ultimately in the hands of the citizens, they create a place where the government is meant to protect and maintain the freedom and the rights of the people for all equally. Our Founders created a completely new form of government and although other countries have implemented aspects of our system there has never been another similar to the American idea.

Our government has since become corrupt; it has grown far beyond what it was ever intended to be. I blame our education for that. Our school systems, especially under common core, have started to subtly teach and favor big government by tainting the history of America. We have been taught lies about our country so upcoming generations think they serve the government rather than the other way around.

Start Your Search:
Watch: projectveritas.com/posts/news/common-core-exec-reveals-anti-american-agenda-guns-stds-islam

Federal control and tainted history is causing a divide in America, a divide of destination. Americans used to want the same outcome for our country, we all agreed on the same basic principles, but younger generations now do not learn those principles. The difference in parties used to be on how we get there not where we're going.

The lack of knowledge when it comes to these principles has a lot to do with the tainted teaching of our founding and the Christian and Biblical influence involved. Our founders drew heavily from their Christian perspective and Biblical studies when writing our founding documents, but schools today overlook this fact and even teach the opposite. Want an example? It's easy enough to find one, just ask yourself how much do you know about the founders Christian influence?

When we do not know the principles, ideas, and mindsets that were instrumental in founding our country we can easily be swayed to false teachings and even opposing ideas. A good example of this is how many people believe that America has a Democratic government when in fact it is a Republic. Although a Democracy and a Republic do not oppose each other the tainted teaching of our founding is fundamentally changing how we view our country today.

Today there are two sides fighting for two outcomes, for the most part Liberals want a bigger more socialist government where varying people groups are treated differently. Liberals want a place where not everything is applied equally but the result is more equal. The Conservatives want the opposite, they want a small republic congruent with the constitution, and the American idea. They want a place where people are equal, all getting treated the same. Conservatives want a place where everything is equally applied but the outcome is up to the individual. This is why we have the Rule of Law, also why we have limited government, and unalienable rights, all of these things are applied the same regardless of race, income, education or heritage. They are meant to provide the same playing field for everyone.

The American dream exists because you have the opportunity, the same opportunity as everyone else, to make something great. The American dream is not simply being great because you are in America. If we compare it to sports: the Conservatives playing field would be a normal field, flat and symmetric. The liberals field would be like a teeter-totter, the winning team would have to spend more energy running uphill while the losing team would have gravity to help them catch up. But once you catch up and become the winning team the teeter-totter flips now you're running up hill.

Big government allows the government to be the ref and control the teeter-totter, that means it can choose a group of people and call them winners even if they aren't and make them always run uphill. This is how the rest of the world has governed for ages and that is why America is important.

America was designed to be an equal playing field

where the players determine the winner not the ref. Our founders created America to be an escape from the overruling refs, a place where you could go to be free and win at life. We have since lost this, our government is growing and shifting the teeter-totter as we speak, we are becoming like the rest of the world, the very place our ancestors ran from.

We must stop this path, reduce government and put it back in the correct spot as a fair, equal ref, creating a place with the same law for all players. That is what made us important to the world, and if we don't return to the country our ancestors designed the world will lose its hope for a "fair game." If it does hundreds of millions of dreams will be crushed as the beautiful stadium is replaced with a teeter-totter. It is time to stop the teeter-totter being built in America and go back to the Constitution, the flat and fair playing field.

KICK START

- Watch Dinesh D'Souza's movie *America: Imagine the world without her.* This documentary is from the perspective of an immigrant and demonstrates what America has done in the past and how it has affected the world in a positive way.
- Do your own research on the positive things America has done and what we need to do to keep that up.
- Think about what makes America unique, what values, ideas, and actions make us different?
- Research what the French researcher Alexis de Tocqueville observed when visiting America in the 1830s.

VALUES

*"When your values are clear to you,
making decisions becomes easier"*
-Ron E Disney

Individual Core Values are what built America. Early Americans had strong values, stuck to them and fought for them, the result of that made our country great. We must continue this but first off we need to know what values are. According to the Oxford dictionary Values are a person's principles or standards of behavior. Basically values are how people judge what is important in life. Values are integrity and willingness to do what is right even when it means pain and sacrifice. Values are what drive true charity, true love, and true sacrifice.

THE IMPORTANCE OF VALUES

Values determine what we stand for and how we build our character. When we have strong core values we have a compass by which to live. Values give us a system for making decisions and for holding others decisions accountable. When we hold good core values and stick to them it creates a better community.

Core Values are the basis of what made America great, but currently our values are fading into materialistic, self-serving rituals. We must go back to the True American values that built this country. America used to lead in the fight for morality and charity, but that all fades away as our values do. America has lead the movement against world hunger, fought in wars that didn't benefit us and revolutionized the way the world thinks about helping your neighbor. We had strong ethical values by which to make our decisions and because of that we believed that it was our duty to help those in need. It didn't matter how big or how small, we sacrificed for others.

Values are important because they give us a strong compass to follow as we make our decisions, a compass that is willing and voluntary. Without them all we are left with is laws on paper and selfish desires that will never really amount to anything. Laws and logical words don't drive us because they lack emotion. The only thing that can set America back on a successful path to leading the world in morality, equality, and charity is the heart and character of every citizen.

That being said the emotion involved in values is not shallow, it is a deep conviction. True Americans stick to their values despite the hardships and don't back down. A perfect example of this is the three Americans that saved the French train from a terrorist in August of 2015. These three Americans did not hesitate to rush a man holding multiple weapons, they saw a need, took responsibility, had courage and got the job done. They risked their lives to save the lives of many others on the train without expecting any reward or honor in return. They did what was right because they have a conviction for True American values.

Every True American has a code of values by which they live. These values go hand in hand with the American idea and resemble what makes the American idea possible. There are six predominant values that were necessary for the creation of America and are still necessary for its success.

Responsibility: Upholding your values and being accountable for the outcome of your decisions. Taking action on your values and decisions. Being responsible is making sacrifices for something larger than yourself and stepping up, without question, when duty calls.

Equality: Believing that "all men are created equal." No person is above another, all have the same rights, they are all under the same law, and they can all achieve. Everyone has the same freedom and the same opportunity. To no person is more given and from no person is more demanded.

Courage: The strength to confront fear head-on, to accept the risks of life and live the life of your dreams. Courage is to stand up for what you believe, making tough choices and persevering despite the hardships.

Independence: The act of taking responsibility for yourself and relying on your own abilities. Independence is to achieve for yourself, rather than rely on what others can do for you. When life strikes you make do with what you have, you master personal skills and find satisfaction in your accomplishments.

Authenticity: Acting on your beliefs, recognizing that you are your own person, and striving to be the best YOU that you can be. Authenticity is saying what you mean, and recognizing your short comings while remembering your strengths.

Honor: Being trust worthy and following through with your word, despite the hardships. Honor is standing for what is ethical, above what is legal. To have honor is to have conviction and integrity.

Are these values familiar or surprising to you? They should be familiar because they built this country, but they are becoming increasingly scares. It is our job to make these values overwhelmingly evident in America once again. If we continue to let these values fade away we will continue to watch our country fall from greatness.

WHY WE NEED THESE VALUES

America is straying from these values because we have become self-focused. During the "Me" generation we lost the most important part of values, Responsibility, and with it went the desire to help others. We have stopped caring about our neighbors and our community. We are so focused on "what can you do for me" and "someone else will help if I don't."

This lost focus on values and new focus on self is shaping our country, and hurting our reputation. We were once known as a country of hard work, generosity, and honesty. While we may still be regarded in such a way, it is fading. Now the common stereo types are fat couch potatoes only interested in a bigger TV and the next IPhone. We are often thought of as arrogant, and ignorant to the rest of the world. Our reputation is fading at the same rate as our values.

We need to get back to our roots before our roots get pulled up completely. Our roots are still there and many of us still hold true to them but we are not consistent. Those who do hold true to them need to instill them in others and challenge those who oppose True American values all together.

We have become complacent thinking "someday they will figure out that they're not the only people on earth." We say to ourselves "they will realize that they have to earn their place in the world." The problem is, they are earning their place in the world, it's just an unsustainable, emotion driven place. We keep fooling ourselves watching more and more people go on food stamps or not move out of their parent's basement. It's not working, we can't stand back and let the rest of our generation and our nation go on like this, we need to be the change, we need to lead by example. We have got to instill a strong passion for America's roots and core values. We must adopt these values as common ground in the fight for a better America. Most importantly we must take up our duty and take Responsibility in every aspect of our lives.

KICK START

- Think about your current Values, do you have a solid set you live by? How are they different than these?

- Take action on these Values, write or type them out and post them on your wall or your fridge, practice them daily and build these values in your own life.

- Share these values with your friends and family, get the word out and challenge them to integrate them into their lives as well

- Reflect on how you have lived your life up to this point have you lived by these values on accident? Reflect on the outcome in your life from the way you have lived and look how these values have or will change the outcome.

- Look for these values in your surroundings, do leaders in your life live by these values? Do the people you interact with practice these values or different values of their own? Do the heroes in your life live by these values or similar ones? Start to take notice of life around you and see how it is prospering and how it is suffering and what values are behind those outcomes.

- Read *Cowboy Values* by James Owen to see how cowboys resemble the True American

RESPONSIBILITY

"We must reject the idea that every time a law is broken, society is guilty rather than the lawbreaker. It is time to restore the American precept that each individual is accountable for his actions"
-Ronald Reagan

The most important value we must hold is responsibility. Responsibility is the glue that holds the rest of our values together and also puts them to action. Being responsible means being the person who causes something to happen. Taking responsibility is what separates the successful from those stuck in turmoil. True Americans have always taken responsibility; they don't lay blame on others or let their circumstances hold them back. True Americans understand that taking responsibility means that you cannot be the victim of your environment. When you are responsible it is always your job to better your situation, and it is your own fault when life is not what you want it to be.

Because Americans take responsibility for their actions they reap the benefits or consequences of those actions and decisions. They realize that they are the ones that made it happen. If the founders of

America did not take responsibility we would not have broken away from England, or created a successful government. As our willingness to take responsibility fades our country goes with it.

RESPONSIBILITY FOR YOURSELF

Taking responsibility includes much more than it sounds like. Taking responsibility means recognizing that you are the person that shapes the outcome and you must take steps to make the outcome great. What do you do when outside factors start to affect you, your family, or your future? Do you blame others who may be involved or do you examine yourself and find places you can improve to better the situation?

You might be thinking "if my significant other (I'm going to shorten that to S/O meaning girlfriend, boyfriend, wife...) is cheating on me, she is to blame for that, I can't control her so that is not my responsibility." Let's use that example, your S/O is a person directly correlated with you that makes her own choices, on the surface it looks like it is not your responsibility. It appears as if you have no control in what she is doing and you had no part in making it happen. Even if that is true it does not excuse you from being responsible for the outcome.

In this example it is your job to do everything you can to remedy the relationship. Let me parallel this to a different circumstance that will be a little more extreme. Say your S/O wasn't cheating on you but rather texting while driving home. She runs a red light and gets hit by another car. When you hear that she has been in an accident what goes through your mind? Are you thinking "if my S/O was dumb enough to run a red light, she is to blame for that, I can't control her so her crash is not my responsibility." Or are you thinking "Maybe the breaks went out because I did the maintenance instead of the shop? Maybe she was rushing because I hounded her about being late to dinner? What do I need to do right now to make sure she will be okay?" I'm guessing you're thinking the latter, although the potential outcome, the loss of your S/O, is the same in both circumstances (although at different levels), and both circumstances are caused by her choices you choose to take responsibility for one but not the other.

Taking responsibility provokes action. When you take responsibility in the example of the car crash you are looking for anything you can do to make it better, but in the example of the affair you blame your S/O for the circumstances and give up, thinking there is nothing that you can do about it. In reality there is more you can do to remedy the affair than the crash, but only if you are going to take responsibility.

Your other response could be to blame the guy she had an affair with saying it's his fault and he is responsible for your failing relationship, that's ridiculous. In the car crash example that would be like blaming the driver that hit her for not seeing her and stopping in time. You would be blaming the one with the green light for your S/O running the red. That sounds crazy right? It should, but that is what it looks like when people do not take responsibility and instead play the blame game.

"So how can I take responsibility when it's something my S/O or family member is deciding to do?" Well look at all the ways that you influence that person. In the affair example this might be caused by your lack of interest in her cooking, or never taking time away from work to be with her, not calling her beautiful...ect. There is almost always a reason a decision is made that could hurt another, and this is usually caused by both parties unwillingness to take responsibility. This is why it is absolutely critical that you take 100% responsibility for yourself, including your relationships and your future. When you don't take 100% responsibility one small incident can escalate into a huge problem from a growing gap of blame.

Now comes the hard one, taking responsibility for your future. This one is hard because it is always happening. Taking responsibility for your future doesn't happen in a few big decisions, it happens in a bunch of little ones. Well a bunch of little ones after the first big one. First of course you need to decide that you will take responsibility for your future.

Almost every decision you make affects your future because of the compound effect. The compound effect explains the outcome of a little choice that over time ends in a big result. This could be as simple as giving up pop and losing weight, or doing a short exercise every day and having a longer life.

> **Start Your Search:**
> Check out *The Compound Effect* By Darren Hardy
> The Compound Effect explains how small, every day decisions create big life changes.

In order to take responsibility for your future you need to know where you want to be in the future. If you don't have a plan or a destination for the outcome of your future than you can't accurately make decisions that will get you there. The first step in taking responsibility for your future comes in the form of a goal or a destination, after you know what you want your end result to be you can start weighing your decisions upon that.

In the case of the Pilgrims their destination was a land where they could be free to practice their religion. So every decision they made revolved around the quest to finding this free land. Obviously their story is a little more drastic than our everyday lives but it shows how you must plan and stick to your values. The Pilgrims knew their mission and decided that they would not stop until they found religious freedom. Throughout all of the extreme decisions and risks they had to take they were courageous, responsible, independent, authentic, and honorable.

The Pilgrims made decisions not only for their own future but also for their families future. They took responsibility for their family by looking at what the future had to offer and making their decisions based upon what their future needed to offer. Their future in England did not offer them freedom so they decided to go to Holland, and when that stopped offering the outcome they desired they went to America.

They took responsibility for their circumstances and because they did they had to make decisions to change their environment. Responsibility lies in every part of our lives. You must take responsibility for yourself because it is your job and your job only. It is your responsibility to shape the outcome of your life as well as your influence and impact on those around you.

TAKE RESPONSIBILITY FOR YOUR COUNTRY

I'm sure by now you understand why taking responsibility is so important to the existence and survival of America but I will expound a little more on what we should be doing to take responsibility for our country. America is supposed to have a government that is of the people by the people and for the people, so what does that mean exactly? It means that we the people of America are responsible for its wellbeing. Ultimately that makes us responsible for not only ourselves but also our fellow citizens and the world since a corrupt America could be very harmful to the world.

It all starts by taking responsibility for yourself which by now you should understand is important. If we can't be responsible for ourselves there is no way we can be responsible for our country. Just like in a relationship when blame is laid on the other person, it goes back and forth growing into an deeply engrained conflict and the same is true for our country. If the poor blame the rich and the user in error blames the manufacturer it will grow into a much larger issue all the while keeping the people who are blaming others for their problems in a downward spiral of failure.

We must take responsibility in our country, or the blame will continue to go back and forth. Fading Americans stopped taking responsibility to the point that they will sue over frivolous things like Red Bull not giving you wings. Obviously the people behind this suit did not take responsibility for themselves or their country. Another example of this could be the

Texas lawsuit in which a drunk woman, intoxicated almost twice over the legal limit, backs into Galveston Bay and drowns due to failure to unbuckle her seatbelt. Her family then sues Honda for poorly designing the seatbelt. In reality it was illegal for this woman to drive in the first place and had she not gone in the bay she would have been a danger to others on the road as well. These lawsuits show how quick some Americans are to lay blame rather than take responsibility. Coincidentally they make America look selfish around the world as we resort to frivolous lawsuits just to make a quick buck.

Taking responsibility for your country means helping out in your community, voting and actually researching who to vote for, and not blaming other people whether it be the government, your community or companies for your problems or the countries problems. If we don't start taking responsibility soon there won't be a great country left to take responsibility for. I'm taking responsibility by writing this book, and you can take responsibility by simply putting the information in this book into action and sharing this book with your friends and family. It's not too late now, don't wait until it is.

KICK START

- Look at all the places in your life you have blamed others knowing there was more you should have done.
- Reflect on how blame has escalated your problems.
- List places in your life where you need to take more responsibility.

DO YOUR OWN

HOMEWORK

"I was bold in the pursuit of knowledge, never fearing to follow truth and reason to whatever results they led, and bearing every authority which stood in their way"
-Thomas Jefferson

You must do your own homework in today's America. Stop listening to the main stream media, stop letting others think for you, and start forming your own thoughts from information you can trust. Today's main stream media is very bias to the left. (aside from Fox news that is which is to the right) You'll notice this when they cover stories or candidates and constantly push a theme. They consistently make the right look evil for everything they do. Yet when the left does something bad they blame it on something else like diversity, inequality, guns, or Christians.

Think critically when listening to the news, look at the writing on the wall, look at the results of the people you are listening to. Do you notice when they tell you more gun control is needed to stop shootings but fail to tell you that the shooting happened in a gun free zone with a gun that was already illegally possessed or possessed by a person with a mental illness? Look at what they're not telling you and don't believe everything you hear. Think for yourself and do your own homework. It's not enough to listen to the news now and then because you cannot trust their stories. You need to know what is actually happening so that you know what you stand for and why you stand for it!

WHY DO YOUR OWN HOMEWORK

Doing your own homework is important because others will tell you what they want you to hear. Sometimes it is true, sometimes it is only partially true and other times it is flat out wrong. When it is not true, they either stand for something they have been told and actually know nothing about, or they are so stuck in their own way of thinking that they don't look at the devastating results of what they stand for.

If they stand for Obamacare and you don't think for yourself from your own homework they are going to tell you everything you need to hear to stand on their side, they may only highlight the good and give you the "promises." In the main stream media's case, for the most part, that is what you would get. Take for instance the most obvious example of this, "If you like your health care plan, you can keep it." Obama said this at least 37 times, yet come 2013 millions of people had their plans cancelled, and were forced to buy more expensive plans or abandon health insurance all together.

Those in favor of Obamacare justified this by

saying their plans were substandard and didn't provide key features "everyone needs" those features include, maternity care, mental health and addiction treatment, rehabilitative services, prescription drugs, and pediatric services. It is pretty obvious grandparents don't need pediatric services and men don't need maternity care, but thanks to Obamacare everyone is required to pay for them on their health insurance plan. You may have bought the justification that the plans were substandard, when in reality all that means is that they don't cover services you will never need.

Start Your Search:
Read: nbcnews.com/news/other /obama-admin-knew-millions-could-not-keep-their-health-insurance-f8C11484394

And: healthcare.gov/blog/10-health-care-benefits-covered-in-the-health-insurance-marketplace/

Often times you'll also get second hand information from someone who also did not do their own homework. Since it sounds good from what they heard they will pass on false information. They will tell you your monthly payment will go down, they'll tell you that you can keep your doctor, and that you can keep your current plan. You will hear about all of the things that make it sound good but we all know that is not how it turned out for many people. Heath care costs rose in high percentages in many areas, for instance in Minnesota costs rose by almost 50%, that means many are dropping coverage to keep the costs manageable. Obamacare is a highly politicized issue and it is hard to find any solid facts that hold up for more than six months. Even still those doing their own homework saw this coming.

So why do you do your own homework? You do your own homework because you cannot trust the information you get the easy way. The mainstream media, your college professors, your friends and even your family will give you information that is either a flat out lie (intentional or not) or so far out of context that it doesn't mean what it originally meant. That's not to say none of these sources can be trusted but do some checking for yourself.

The reason people fall for misinformation is because they have nothing to weigh it against. They have no comparison and no context. You need to have an understanding of what is viable and what is not. Many things sound good because you don't know what the alternative is.

Take for example diversity, the American idea that makes our country unique creates the melting pot that we are. Under the American idea you become and are regarded to as an "American" when you become an American citizen. It does not depend on ethnicity or heritage, but rather it becomes apparent through your mindset. In other countries you would likely be regarded as your ethnicity for generations. You may be a citizen of that country but you are not regarded as carrier of its heritage. When immigrating to America and perusing the American dream not only can you become an American citizen but you would also be regarded as an "American" carrying on Americas heritage as equal with those born here.

This is where E Pluribus Unum comes in as part

of the American idea. E Pluribus Unum means "From many, One" Widely known as referring to the idea of our governmental system, from many states we form one country. Just as it describes the idea of our government it also describes the idea of the "American" as we talked about above. The first committee created to design the nations Great Seal, made up of Franklin, Adams, and Jefferson along with Pierre Eugène Du Simitère as the artist. They designed a seal saying "E Pluribus Unum" underneath with a shield in the middle having six symbols representing the six countries, from which the American colonies were populated. These countries were England as a rose, Scotland as a thistle, Ireland as a harp, France as Fleur-de-lis, Holland as the Belgic lion, and Germany as an imperial eagle. Although their design was not accepted the phrase was, this shows us what the main founding fathers intended E Pluribus Unum to mean and it is what makes America an idea rather than merely a country.

Now let's look at diversity today. America has had many issues with race in the past but we have also had many victories. Sadly today we are undermining those victories and going backwards. Race has become the focus of the media, the schools, and activist groups and it is not helping the cause. By consistently talking about race and diversity, insisting it is still a huge oppressive problem we are creating a huge oppressive problem. If we were to actually adhere to the American idea we could be a country of American people not a country of diverse ethnicities all trying to coexist. Liberal diversity may mean well but the outcome is only leading to more separation due to the different labels, so called micro aggressions, affirmative action and so on, this is undermining the value of E Pluribus Unum.

Today we are told to constantly think of race and place everyone in these stereo typed boxes of race or sexual orientation so we can treat them differently because of their "disadvantage" or vice versa. When we are all just Americans it doesn't matter what race you are because you are like me, an American, and that is how it is supposed to be. Maybe you're a different color, sex, orientation, or class but we value freedom, we value opportunity, we value equal rights, and we value the rule of law. But now we are told we do not value the same things, and sometimes even tricked into valuing the opposite creating a divide between us and a war for what we're told to stand for.

Where there is a strong common goal there is a connection that can overcome prejudices. A perfect example of this can be seen in the true story movie *Remember the Titans*, a white and a black school come together and the football team is forced to integrate. As they are regarded as equal, forced to interact as individuals, led by good example, and set on a common goal they overcome their prejudice and become a very successful team.

Start Your Search:
Read: psychologytoday.com/blog/psychologist-the-movies/201211/remember-the-titans-can-football-reduce-racism

Today there should be no reason that any race should be disadvantaged. Take for instance the first woman self-made millionaire, Madam C.J. Walker, a black woman, in fact she was the first free born in her family. She could make herself a millionaire back in the early 1900s and the richest person on tv today is Oprah Winfrey, who, by the way is not only the richest of all tv show hosts but she is three times richer than the next 9 richest hosts combined. It is not the color of your skin that holds you back, it is your mindset. Today race is not the determining factor, what you believe about your race is. Today minorities are consistently being told that they don't have the same opportunities and therefore need the handouts the Left will give them. Minorities are not held down in America they are told they are and when they believe that it creates a self-fulfilling prophesy and becomes true.

America is not supposed to be a place where we pity different people groups, it's supposed to be a place where every people group has the same freedom to create the life they want by working hard and making good decisions. That is what the American idea is meant to create but it is being undermined by this modern diversity nonsense. Now we give special opportunities to different groups and make small misunderstanding into all out race wars. We need to change our perspective and look at every American citizen as an American seeking a dream of a better life for themselves and those around them.

We need to do our own homework and think critically so we pick up on what is really going on. We need to do our own research on the major issues and candidates for office in our country. We also need to know what effects a law or government program will have on the country, and the Constitutionality of it. In the case of Obamacare it can be disregarded on

Constitutionality alone. The federal government does not have the power to force anyone into commerce like they have with Obamacare. The word-trickery used in the 2012 5/4 Supreme Court decision to make Obamacare Constitutional was a clear sign of its un-Constitutional roots. The individual mandate, requiring you to buy healthcare or get fined, was argued to be called a "fine" for both political and technical reasons, yet for Constitutional purposes it was regarded as a "tax" in the Supreme court decision.

> ## Start Your Search:
> **Read:** discoverthenetworks.org/
> viewSubCategory.asp?id=1957#LEGAL
> CHALLENGESTOOBAMACARE

This should have been a massive red flag that everyone was paying attention to, everyone should have done their own homework on this and looked at what logical effects it would have on the country and governments power in the future. Yet many stood behind it saying it would be great for everyone because current healthcare plans are rip-offs. I think we can all agree it is a far bigger rip-off when you don't have the choice to opt out.

For those of you who do watch mainstream media and think that the information they are giving you is true you need to start thinking about what they say critically. Next time you hear a soundbite or a quote of a presidential candidate look up the real quote or real facts and read all that was left out to make you believe the candidate said and meant something different. You'll be amazed at how much context can be left out.

A perfect example of this is the gun control debate. Context is almost always left out when forwarding gun control but the way it is presented makes gun ownership look evil. Watch the video below to see how they leave out context. Don't fall for the contextless story, you are smarter than that, just put in a little bit of effort and find the real story.

> ### Start Your Search:
> **Watch:** Gun Control Propaganda Debunked
> youtube.com/watch?v=IULSD8VwXEs

HOW DO I START

Doing your own homework isn't really all that time consuming as long as you do it right. In order to do that you first need to find at least three good sources of information, so to find those let's break it down into three easy steps.

#1: Look at the track record of the source. Did they talk about the possible outcomes of a new law or candidate? Where their predictions right? Did they give you reasons why something was good or bad and did those reasons actually matter and add up? Look back at an old story about something that you know the outcome of like the Obamacare example. Find a story from your source that was before Obamacare was passed, did it praise Obamacare or point out its huge flaws? Look at their take on it and look at where it is now, were they right? You need to ask these questions and analyze them closely because if they were consistently wrong and bias on a point until it was undeniable they are not a good source of information.

#2: Look at their criticism. A good news source criticizes everyone about one thing or another, if they aren't criticizing one group of people but are continuously criticizing another they are biased and unreliable. The purpose of a good news source is to ask the tough questions and find the truth and the flaws in every candidate, policy, or story. Then point out the flaws for us to see, and do so in an objective manner. News sources should give you the facts so you can form your own conclusions. That is why the mainstream media is not trustworthy, they hardly ever criticize liberal candidates or policies until after those candidates or policies have totally failed. They also ask very shallow surface questions when in an interview so they don't get the real information or facts that we are looking for.

#3: Look at what they are covering. Are they covering the real issues in our country or are they doing stories that don't have any real significance? Are they talking about a shallow story while other news sources are covering important stories? Look at the stories and you will know real quick what sources are actually bringing you news. Most mainstream news outlets today are just focused on the ratings. They are entertainment stations not information stations. For a perfect example just look at the disproportionate amount of time the media is giving Trump. Trump gets ratings, good ones, so he was in the headlines almost every day in the 2016 primaries.

Once you have found your three good sources and know they are reliable you need to use them! Spend a few minutes every week to read a little bit about the biggest things going on in our county, whether it be for the presidential campaign, policy changes, new laws, or tragic events. Once you know what is going on you can decide if it is something that you need to do some more research on or if it's just adding to an earlier story.

When it comes to policies and candidates you also need to review and compare them against the Constitution, are they Constitutional or do they go against the governments given authority? (Check out the back of the book to read the Constitution.)

Remember to challenge the media don't take everything they say as truth, think critically. If they are advocating for more government subsidies but then saying taxes will go down as a result, don't take their word for it. What they have just told you is 4=1, now I know you would not fall for that so why would you fall for more government spending equals no tax increase? Start to think about what they are telling you logically like this, if the government is going to give you something for free, your neighbor is paying for it with his taxes. Laws can't make things cheaper, and cheaper to the consumer does not equal cheaper for the tax payer.

HISTORY

The best news source is history. You may have been told that history doesn't apply to our day and age well guess what, it does. History repeats itself and it won't stop doing so until we actually look at it and figure out what happened before.

*"Study history, study history. In history lie all
the secrets of statecraft."
Winston Churchill, May 27, 1953*

America is not exempt to losing its freedom, its wealth, or its opportunity. Our country will lose everything that makes it great if we don't wake up and start taking action against what's destroying it.

When you're considering how to vote look at history because chances are in the past there has been a similar law or leader (either here or some other country) and it shaped their future, so figure out if that future was good or bad. For example, look at every mass genocide, gun control was always a prerequisite to mass genocide. Nazi Germany prohibited Jews from owning guns to ease the killing of millions of Jews. Also look at the strict gun laws in the Soviet Union making possible the forced famine of 1933 killing an estimated 7 million Ukraine farmers.

Start Your Search:
Read: mises.org/library/gun-control-nazi-germany

And: thenewamerican.com/culture/history/item/4656-holodomor-the-secret-holocaust-in-ukraine

History often holds the answers to how a new policy will turn out and how it will affect our country so remember to look at history as a definite source of information pertaining to national decisions. Don't forget to think critically of the history you find though because history can be very bias and tainted as well.

KICKSTART

- Think critically about the news you hear
- Get information from various viewpoints don't solely rely on any one source, like social media, main stream media, or blog sites.
- Always dig deeper than the soundbite/headline

VOTE

"Always vote for principle, though you may vote alone,
and you may cherish the sweetest reflection
that your vote is never lost"
-John Quincy Adams

Voting is one of the most universal ways to participate in our government and our Country's future. It is a very important aspect of being an American and the easiest way to take responsibility and fulfil your duty as an American citizen. In the past when someone couldn't vote it was a big deal, take for instance the women's rights movement, they fought for thirty years for their right to vote. Today we seem to have forgotten that voting is a big deal, according to the census burro only 38% of citizens from 18-24 voted in 2012, and only about 60% of all legal voters actually vote every election cycle. This is crazy to me, 40% of all voters choose not to participate, and less than 50% of young people care to take responsibility for the future of their country by voting.

Voting is a responsibility of being American, we are a country Of the people For the people and By the people and if we don't take responsibility by voting how can we be a country of, for, and by the people?

DECIDING WHO TO VOTE FOR

Deciding who to vote for is one of the most important things you have to do every two years or at least every four years. When looking at candidates and who you should vote for, consider three things.

1. **Their record**
   a. Were they ethical?
   b. Did they get results?
   c. Do they waver on the issues?
2. **Who surrounds them**
   a. What kind of people are on their team?
   b. How are they funded?
3. **Their values**
   a. Are they focused on the future of the country?
   b. Are they focused on fixing the problems or the symptoms?
   c. Are they consistent and clear with their values?

THEIR RECORD

Looking at a candidate's record is always the first thing you should do when considering where to place your vote. Their record will tell you about what kind of person they are, and sometimes it will instantly rule them out. I'm not talking about their criminal record, although if they have one it's definitely a red flag, I'm talking about their past decisions, accomplishments, and failures. What did they do in the past, and is that what you want to see them do once elected?

Ethics are the first thing you should look at on the candidate's record. Do they keep their word? Have they been caught doing something fraudulent? Do they treat others with respect?

Take for example a couple of the presidential candidates for the 2016 presidential primary, we've got Hillary Clinton and Ben Carson. If we look at the records of Hillary Clinton we can quickly rule her out on account of her ethics. There are multiple cases of her boldly lying to the American people, just a couple recent examples are Benghazi and her email server.

It has come out that she did know what was happening during the attack in Benghazi yet she blamed the attack on an internet video. At the hearing she said "what difference at this point does it make" She deliberately told the public something different than what we can read in her emails from the time. Her email server was found to have numerous classified documents and highly sensitive material that she tried to cover up by deleting everything on her server. When asked about whipping (deleting) her server she responded, "What like with a cloth?" She does not act respectfully and she says whatever the people want to hear. On her ethics alone everyone should know that she is not fit to be president.

On the other hand if we look at Ben Carson in the same matter we find that he has kept his word and he is honest. He does not over hype what he has accomplished and he doesn't lie about things in his past or his present. The biggest "lie" the media can find on Carson is about his "scholarship to West Point" which at its worst would boil down to an exaggeration on something little more than an imperfect memory from upwards of forty years ago. Although it is not even an imperfect memory, Politifact proved Politico wrong and found that Carson was indeed correct that West Point did use the words "full scholarship" on their website and in advertising materials. Although it is true that technically you cannot get a "full scholarship" because everyone gets a free ride, West Point does use that language. "Full scholarship" gets the point across much easier and more concise than a lengthy explanation of the actual funding process.

These examples also clearly show the accuracy of the media. There are plenty of news sources defending Hillary's handling of classified secrets, as well as many blowing Carson's "lie" way out of proportion. If you take a step back and look at these situations they aren't in the same league but when reading the stories, they can appear to carry equal weight.

Results should be the second thing you check. Look at their past and what they have accomplished. Did they accomplish what they said they would? Were they successful in their business?

Look at the candidate's accomplishments to see what they will accomplish in the future. If a candidate was in office previously and did not accomplish what they promised then they likely will not accomplish what they promise in the future either. Results are much more important than words. Anyone can say they have a plan, give great solutions, and promise to do it, but very few actually get it done. You can pick out who will actually accomplish what they promise by looking at what they accomplished in their past. If they are promising a better economy and have no business or economic experience how can you trust their claim? The ones who were successful in the past have the determination, passion, and the skills to be successful, the ones that were not, are often doing it for the wrong reasons.

Standings in the candidate's past will show their future stance. Have they changed what they stand for multiple times? Does it seem to reflect special interest groups with lots of money? Are they consistent in what they fight for?

This is a very important part of their past because it shows you their integrity. If they change what they stand for every few years depending on what is best for them at the time or what will earn them the most votes then they do not have integrity. When they don't have integrity they won't follow through with what they promise. Their incentive is not what they believe or truly stand for, it's selfishness, money, or popularity. Often times we elect someone because we like what they stand for and what they promise to accomplish, but after they are elected they work on things that contradict what they said they stand for, and they don't accomplish what they promised. If we look at their past and determine their integrity we will know if they will follow through.

WHO SURROUNDS THEM

The people that a candidate is around the most will

reflect the candidate. This is true for anyone, the people you are with will rub off on you until you are a reflection of them. The saying "You are what you eat" is true when it comes to the people you surround yourself with. If you put junk in you'll get junk out.

"Bad company corrupts good character"
1 Corinthians 15:33 (NIV)

Friends are a window into a candidates true character. Who do they spend time with, do they hang out with other elected officials who's records and accomplishments you can look at? What are their friends involved in? How do the people on their team promote them?

It's not easy to find information on a candidate's friends and acquaintances, but when you can it provides a great insight into what they really stand for. When you can look at what those people have done in the past you can get a better idea of what that candidate is actually working toward regardless of what they say.

You should also look at how their team acts and treats people. Is their team putting out advertisements and information that is helpful to you and your knowledge of the candidate or are they bitterly attacking? This provides great insight to both the candidate and the teams strategy in the campaign. If the people on the campaign team are not the kind of people you want in office then the candidate isn't either.

Investors also reveal a candidates real intentions. Investors are often a lot easier to research than a candidates team but it is not always all that easy to know what kind of agenda that investor might have. Investors sadly make up a huge part of our government system now because our politicians have lost their integrity and dedication for our country and have started catering to the money and personal agendas of those who will pay them. Politicians are often more interested in getting re-elected then doing a good job while they are in office.

Look at who has invested in the candidate, is it a billionaire that wants regulations to cut out smaller companies and up his business? Is it a previous official that wants to stay in control? Investors can be hard to figure out sometimes but make sure to take a look regardless.

THEIR VALUES

Values are very important when considering a candidate. Values drive a person, a person without good strong values cannot be a good leader. When a candidate does not have strong and apparent values they are unpredictable and not trust worthy. Always look at their values before standing behind them.

The first thing you can do when considering their values is to asses them for True American values like we talked about in chapter 6 *Values*. Do they possess these fundamental American values? If they don't it's a good sign that they should not be elected as any kind of leader in American government.

Focus is the second thing to look at. Is their focus on the people? Are they running to represent you and me and the interests of the American people or are they running for selfish reasons?

Every politician should be focused on helping others, serving their country and representing the American people. Politicians should be like soldiers putting aside their differences and working together to represent and defend the American dream of freedom. If politicians acted like soldiers we would not be where we are today, there would not be parties that are so divided that they can't agree on a single thing. There would not be a focus on getting re-elected or liked by other politicians and minority groups.

The focus would be on protecting the freedom of America and serving the country. There would be cooperation and problem solving for everyone including the minority groups. We wouldn't be divided due to race or sex because there would be a common goal, to make the country we love great and solve real problems in effective ways.

Once you see where their values lie you can better understand how they want to fix something. Do they want to fix the **Symptom,** or the **Problem?** Fixing the symptom is popular in the moment and helps with re-election but causes detrimental pain later on. Whereas fixing the actual problem can be painful in the moment but much more rewarding for the whole country down the road.

Our welfare system is currently just treating the symptom of poverty it is not truly helping people get out of poverty it is only helping people in poverty stay in poverty. Candidates focus on fixing the symptoms of a problem because they are either unqualified to solve the actual problem or because they want to be popular for re-election. To solve poverty we have only been treating the symptom by adding more programs and giving more welfare. The Liberal candidates want to extend that even farther, raising taxes on the rich and giving more free and subsidized things to the poor. This is just masking the problem and treating the symptom. It makes these candidates extremely popular to those who receive these benefits and to those who think free assistance fixes the problem. But it doesn't, it just makes it bigger by making more people dependent and pitying those who do not need or want pity. Many want to get away from this reliance on government but can't. The way the system is set up you are almost penalized for getting a job.

Fixing the actual problem is often more difficult because it does not provide the same instant relief that handing out more free benefits does. The problem with just treating the symptom is that it needs constant attention and more and more funding. On the other hand when you solve the actual problem you take away the need to revisit it later. In order to solve the actual problem you cannot keep doing what isn't working.

In 1964 President Johnson started the "War on Poverty" to solve the problem. Sadly fifty two years later the problem still has not been solved. The solution to this problem is to get these people to be self-sufficient so that they no longer need government aid right? What have we done so far to try and accomplish this? We have provided more government aid without requiring much in return. Now just think about that for a second, it sounds counter intuitive right? Well we can prove that it doesn't work because the percentage of people that are not self-sufficient has more or less stayed flat. It rises and falls a couple of percent with the economy but when you take into account the fact that we have spent upwards of $22 trillion to abolish poverty over the past half a century, more government programs hasn't made a difference at all.

So why do we keep doing more of it and expecting it to work? Well, because the people advocating for more of it want to be popular to those who receive it. That is why we have not started to solve the real problem. In order to solve the real problem we need to do the unpopular thing and get welfare recipients back to work and back to providing for themselves.

The solution that requires more effort is always the least popular one among those affected yet it's the one that will actually fix their problem. This is why candidates work on the symptom rather than the cause. Think of the future and make sure your backing the candidate that will solve the cause not the symptom.

Lastly the **Consistency** of their values must be considered. This goes back to looking at their past to see if their values change often, or if they consistently live by them. If you did the looking into their past already you should have noticed how well they stuck to their values. Look at if their decisions and actions are consistent. Do their actions match what they are telling you they stand for? Do they walk their talk and practice what they preach?

If they truly stand behind the values they tell you about they will live by them in their daily life. A good example of this would be the correlation of welfare and charity. If the candidate is campaigning on expanding welfare and helping the poor then logically they should give a lot to charity in their personal life, right? If they aren't giving up their personal money to help the poor what makes them worthy of giving your tax dollars to the poor?

Simply look at how they have lived their life, their values should shine right through. Their values should match their reason for running and the actions they take.

Voting is an essential part of being a True American. When you vote you take responsibility for your country by helping choose the best people to represent us and protect our rights. It is very important to know who we are electing and that we are electing someone that is fit for the job. That is why we must all take the time to do our own research and be involved before voting. Know when your caucuses or primaries are and be involved, don't wait till the general election, be a part of the whole process so we can select the best person for the job.

KICK START

- Do a quick google search on their record, look at what their past holds.
  - Were they ethical?
  - Did they get results and accomplish what they promised?
  - Have they changed what they stand for more than a couple times?
- Look at who they surround themselves with.
  - Can you look at their friends pasts?
  - Who is funding them?
  - How do the people they surround themselves with act?
- Look at their Values.
  - Are they focused on serving you or themselves?
  - Do they want to fix problems or treat symptoms?
  - Do they stand strong in their values or do they waiver?
  - Do they practice what they preach?
- How to find the truth
  - Do some reading on them
  - Look at multiple sources for the same subject
  - Weigh the information on importance
  - Look at their character
  - Try and find the most objective sources possible

DON'T FEED THE

SEAGULLS

"It is the working man who is the happy man. It is the
idle man who is the miserable man"
-Benjamin Franklin

Welfare, the biggest killer of the American spirit and the greatest expense to the American taxpayer. Current welfare is consuming people, and creating a "poverty class" in America. This class of people is becoming more and more reliant on others for their problems and many have forgotten how to be responsible for themselves. Welfare needs to be earned before its recipients can actually rise out of poverty.

Have you noticed the signs at waterfront restaurants that say "DON'T FEED THE SEAGULLS?" Do you know why they put up those signs? When we feed the seagulls they start expecting and relying on being fed in these areas. The more we feed the seagulls the more seagulls come looking for food. Over time this creates a pest problem and hurts business at that restaurant. The same thing applies for welfare. The more welfare that is available the more people sign up to get it, as this happens they become dependent on it and before you know it we have a problem. "Feeding the Seagulls" soon creates too many relying on welfare and not enough paying for it.

CURRENT WELFARE IS KILLING AMERICA

Welfare is drowning America in debt and creating an ever growing class of people that add to the debt rather than contribute to pay it off. Welfare spending is 16 times greater than it was in 1964, we currently spend upwards of one Trillion dollars a year on the eighty plus welfare programs we have.

Now let me define welfare quick because if you go online and search how much is spent on welfare a year almost all of the main stream media will tell you it's a number more like 220 billion. So why the difference? The liberal media defines welfare as only cash benefits like the *Earned Income Tax Credit, Temporary Assistance for Needy Families, Food Stamps,* and *Housing vouchers.* In reality welfare should be defined by any government benefit given to a specific economic class of people, the government calls these "Means Tested" programs. When you define it like that Medicare, Medicaid, Head Start, Title 1 Grants, Low Income Taxpayer Clinics, and other means tested programs are welfare. Once you add up all the benefits only available to those in "poverty" it comes to around a trillion a year.

What's worse than the fact that welfare is growing at astonishing rates is that it doesn't actually help the majority of its recipients. Our current welfare system is addictive, you can get the equivalent of $20 an hour for doing nothing and that creates a bunch of people who don't want to do anything. Jobs equivalent to that pay would be Plumbers, Electricians, Mechanics, Interior designers, and so on. These jobs don't require very much education, all you need is a little skill and some hard work, but when you can get the equivalent handed to you it's easy to see where the problem lies.

Welfare destroys the people who use it because they become reliant, they don't take responsibility for themselves and in the younger generations they become entitled.

Welfare destroys the need to learn, adapt, and problem solve. It lets you sit around and wait for your circumstances to perfectly cater to your needs. It takes away the urgency to figure out how to be valuable in the marketplace and solve the problem of how to provide for your own needs. This just makes these people less employable because of their lack of ability to learn and adapt. It also creates an attitude of reliance, people start to get comfortable not earning and they start relying on the system and expecting others to help them more and more as they get more and more comfortable.

When people grow up in an environment where they do not need to earn money they develop an attitude of entitlement. This is true for people growing up on welfare as well as kids that are not expected to work or move out of the house as they grow up. When someone is given something for nothing for an extended period of time they start to take it for granted, creating an entitled mindset.

This mindset is detrimental when it comes time for them to actually provide for themselves because they expect it to be easy and they expect things to be given to them. Entitled kids don't understand that they are responsible for providing for themselves, and in order to do that you must be valuable to the market, either with skills or a product. Continuous welfare just reinforces an "it's about me" belief creating a growing class of entitled adults that don't understand that you earn by doing things for others not the other way around.

There are cases when welfare is needed, say you were injured, sick, or a single mom with a new baby. In these cases it is likely you would need some sort of welfare, the problem comes when it is no longer needed but still used. This is where American values need to step in and you need to be courageous taking responsibility to be independent and self-sufficient. You need to have honor by earning your own way despite legally being eligible for government handouts.

Current welfare, and the lack of American values is creating more people to spend the money and less to pay it off. It is raising debt and therefore taxes which is crushing small business owners and the middle class. In the long run all this will do is create more people that will use government benefits. Welfare does not work when it is free, welfare without work = more welfare and a larger "poverty class."

HOW SHOULD IT WORK

Welfare should not be a federal endeavor. Of course there will always be a need for some government aid such as disability but there should not be long term government paid housing, food, or health care. Welfare should be done directly by the community through local churches and local community organizations.

This would work better in the long run by holding people accountable and connecting them with people who can help. Doing welfare this way also gives them more incentive to start earning for themselves by having personal knowledge of where their help comes from. Part of what makes the welfare system so broken is how easy it is to abuse because of how disconnected it is. When we create a connection between those serving and those being served they have an example to learn from as well as more urgency.

Our welfare system pushes the people receiving it into a community of a bunch of other people who are also receiving it. When they are surrounded by likeminded people how can they ever break loose and gain a mindset of success, self-sufficiency, and problem solving? When they are around a bunch of other people who are comfortable relying on others, they will never have the influence or guidance to break loose and achieve more.

Currently welfare is set up so that the people who are self-sufficient pay higher taxes which is then distributed by the government to people who do not know how to be self-sufficient. This means that the person in poverty has no interaction with the one paying for his welfare. This is one instance where the great divide between the rich and the poor is created. The poor man resents the rich man because he has all the stuff and the freedom, and the rich man despises the poor man because he subsidizes the poor man's life through high taxes.

Welfare needs to be a more personal endeavor,

and require more work. More interaction with the ones paying, whether it be a church or organization, would cut down on long-term welfare. The interaction between the recipient and the funder will give the recipient more incentive to become self-sufficient faster. When welfare comes through tax credits, food stamps, and subsidized housing the urgency is lost, sure there may be a deadline or a cut off but when you can make more money, easier, through welfare than at an entry-level job, the number of people working to become self-sufficient before that deadline is slim.

Currently there is around 94 million people who are not in the workforce at all, that means they are neither employed nor looking for a job. Of that about 44 million are between the ages of 20-64. In 2015 we hit a 38 year low in labor force participation with a little over 62% participation. Americas work ethic is fading and as it does our country falls farther and farther in debt. Conversely the federal government gets more and more power.

Our welfare system needs to require work, and provide more incentive to get back in the work force. The longer we let our welfare system grow the harder it will be to fix; we need to once again become a country of doers. Our current welfare system leads to socialism, it takes away urgency and responsibility thus promoting more government control. That is the complete opposite of what built America and if we don't fix our welfare system soon it will drive America even further into mediocrity.

KICK START

- Look at how welfare is working in your community
- Volunteer in your community to help those in poverty break out of it.
- Vote for officials that want to cut back on the current welfare system and fix its shortfalls.

AMERICA'S

FOUNDATION

*"Our Constitution was made only for a moral and
religious people. It is wholly inadequate to the
government of any other"*
-John Adams

America was created from the idea you can see on
every U.S. coin but in order for the three parts of that
idea to thrive it needs three principle foundations.
These foundations provide the basis of what has
allowed America to become great and, when
removed, will lead to America's fall. The foundation
of the United States of America is made up of strong
Biblical Values, **Natural order** and the **Founding
documents** which create a legal system that defends
the other two foundations.

These foundations create the land of the free
where you can aspire to be whatever you want. Upon
this foundation a country that provides a fair and
equal playing field emerged for all. This foundation is
worth fighting for, it made America great in the
beginning and it can make America great again.

CHRISTIAN ROOTS

Biblical teachings and Christianity are being shunned in America today. Many schools and universities are trying to suppress the history that our country was built on Christian and Biblical principles. They leave out that our founders were believers in God. That's all fine and dandy if you want a mediocre country that insists on changing its own history to support the lie of what America was.

It is undeniable that America was built on Christian values, it is baked into our history. America is known for being generous, accepting, and trustworthy, at least it used to be. The Declaration of Independence references God four times, many of our courthouses have the 10 commandments, the Bible was used in our schools till 1963, the New England Primer taught kids to read with Biblical principles for 150 years. More apparent today our money says "In God We Trust", and many of our monuments have references to God for instance the Jefferson Memorial, the Washington Monument and the Lincoln Memorial just to name a few. Let's not forget that the oldest and most successful schools in the country, Harvard, Yale, Princeton were all founded as Christian schools even before Americas founding.

God is referenced time and time again through America's history. He is often acknowledged and thanked for our great victories and our many blessings. Yet in the past sixty years our Christian heritage has been fading to the point where it is now a question to whether America was founded on any

Christian principals or values. We have been fed lies about our history for more than half a century and have now gotten to the point where the lies are a widespread belief.

I'm not going to make this chapter a collection of examples because I want you to go out and see it for yourself. The reason God can get kicked out of this country is because we have gotten so used to being spoon fed our information. If we checked the facts for ourselves we would not be led astray as we have.

Believe it or not the founding fathers were for the most part Christians, even those who were not firm believers were proponents of Jesus's morals. This is pretty evident in the documents we can read from Congress. Read them for yourself at www.loc.gov/exhibits/religion/. Also look at the Jefferson bible for example, Jefferson may not have been any more than a deist but he definitely supported Jesus's teachings. (A deist believes there is a divine creator but that he does not intervene in human affairs.)

FOUNDATION OF BIBLICAL PRINCIPLES

There are a few main Biblical principles that played a big part in making America the great nation it is known as today. Those main principals are:

- Individual Responsibility
- Integrity
- Acceptance
- Generosity

These principals are portrayed all throughout the

Bible and are very important to the way that we should live. It is also very evident how much these principles play a part in Americas history.

Individual Responsibility is the most important Biblical principle practiced in America. Without this principle our capitalist system falls apart, our government grows, and our freedom vanishes.

Individual Responsibility is what allows us to have Individual Liberty. When we are not responsible for ourselves from a decision standpoint our government feels the need to add new laws and regulations prohibiting us from making those decisions. A parallel to this would be like partying as a teenager.

Say you use the individual liberty your parents gave you to go to a party, you end up getting drunk and don't get home till the morning. When your parent ask where you were your honest with them but you blame getting drunk on your friends. Your parents then decide that the whole house needs an 10pm curfew and that you can't go out at night with those friends anymore. Your irresponsibility evoked your parents to put in place new rules not only for you and your friends but also your siblings. You sacrificed your individual liberty by being irresponsible. The difference between the parents in this example and the government is that you never get to grow out of the governments laws and regulations.

On a different front having individual responsibility contributes to being more productive. Capitalism thrived in America because we coupled our own self-interest with self-responsibility. We provided for ourselves and took responsibility for our success and our failure. Individual responsibility doesn't play the blame game, when we are responsible for ourselves we know that our lives and our futures are dependent on us. By coupling this belief in responsibly with self-interest we've combined consequences and morals, with the motivation of reward. This potent combination is necessary for an economically and socially thriving America.

The Bible talks about taking individual responsibility. It teaches that you must work and be responsible to be successful. Take these verses for example, they talk about not only being self-sufficient but also sharing your earnings with those in need.

"Even while we were with you, we gave you this command: 'those unwilling to work will not get to eat.' "
2 Thessalonians 3:10 (NLT)

"If you are a thief, quit stealing. Instead, use your hands for good hard work, and then give generously to others in need."
Ephesians 4:28 (NLT)

The last major factor that makes individual responsibility so important is the sense of morality it gives us. When we are acting responsibly we are not just doing what is best for us but also what is best for those around us. When we provide for ourselves it lifts that burden off of the community around us, and puts us in a position to help. Likewise when we are making responsible decisions we are not only saving ourselves a lot of trouble in the future but also those around us that would be affected by our decisions.

Individual responsibility is one of the corner stones of America's foundation due to the big role it plays in everything from economics to family life.

Sadly these days we are not taking responsibility like we should. As we talked about in chapter six *Responsibility* we need to start taking responsibility in every part of our lives. Americans used to take responsibility for everything they did, and that greatly contributed to their freedom, their morals, and their success. In order to be a true American and make America great once again we must take our Individual Responsibility seriously.

Integrity is another Biblical principle that America is losing quickly. Americans used to honor their word and speak truthfully. Our media used to work for the people, getting out real stories without the political bias against guns, free speech, and the free market. Our politicians even used to be trustworthy, just imagine if we held Obama to the same integrity standard we held Nixon, he would have been impeached upwards of fifteen times over. Integrity is a crucial part of who we are but today it has faded to the point that we cannot rely on our media or our government anymore.

> **Start Your Search:**
> **Read:** 25 Laws broken by Obama, committeeforjustice.org/content/25-violations-law-president-obama-and-his-administration

The Bible speaks a lot about honesty and Integrity, and our founders lived by these principles. Without integrity we will always end up with a corrupt and over powering government. We must instill integrity in our lives and our families lives, it is crucial if we want to keep our freedom.

"Honesty guides good people; dishonesty destroys treacherous people."
Proverbs 11:3 (NLT)

Although many Americans still have integrity; our schools, our media and our government have lost that integrity. As a country we are being misled and brought down by the "treacherous" people we have elected. Luckily there are still a few in Washington that have integrity but they are far and few between. There are far more dishonest people on Capitol Hill then there should be and we need to start taking notice of this and holding them accountable for their actions.

"Just say a simple, 'Yes, I will,' or 'No I won't.' Anything beyond this is from the evil one."
Matthew 5:37 (NLT)

We are also losing our integrity by not sticking to our word, how often do you offer your help to someone without ever intending on actually following through? When the time comes we say we're busy and try to dodge what we previously committed to. This is getting more and more common and it is destroying our sense of community and self-sacrifice.

"I know that you are pleased with me, for my enemy does not triumph over me. Because of my integrity you uphold me…"
Psalm 41:11-12 (NIV)

This verse really knocks us off our feet, how far

have we come from upholding Gods ethics with integrity? How often do we dismiss unethical movements or agendas that are bringing our country away from honoring the God that inspired its creation and success? How often do we let our integrity slide because we are too selfishly occupied with our everyday lives? If we do not regain our integrity both individually and as a country the "enemy" will triumph over us.

Acceptance is a Christian value that truly makes America special. This one is so special that it earned its own spot in the American idea. (If you haven't guessed yet I'm talking about E Pluribus Unum) Think about who makes up America? People from all over the world, people come from just about every country on earth to be American. They come to find the American dream and freedom from their oppressive countries.

People want to be Americans because they like the values we hold and freedom that allows us to make our ambitions a reality. New Americans aren't coming to change our culture or get special handouts they are coming to build a better future for their family and become a part of the American culture of freedom, ambition, and dreams. America has always been very accepting of these people on the one condition that they come to assimilate and become "American." (What I mean by this is that they learn English, share our core values, and seek the American dream.) We believe that God created all people equal, all who truly want to live the American dream should be welcome.

The Bible teaches us to be accepting and forgiving

of one another. We should not be divided for our differences but rather accepting and united in our commonalities.

> *"Always be humble and gentle. Be patient with each other, making allowance for each other's faults because of your love. Make every effort to keep yourselves united in Spirit, binding yourselves together with peace."*
> Ephesians 4:2-3 (NLT)

This shows us what is necessary for the successful acceptance of people from another culture, be patient and humble. Be united as American's and hold yourselves together with likeminded values and principles. (Yes I know that it is originally pertaining to the church but the same idea applies for America)

America has done a very good job of being accepting and patient towards each other, if we weren't we would not be able to have a culture that accepts anyone but still creates a unique and united culture. Sure there are still some who are racist and don't look past their differences but that is unavoidable because we value individual freedom. The rest of us banded together as Americans, we looked past all of our other differences and we prospered greatly for it.

Generosity is one area where the USA has excelled above every other country sadly that is declining now. Until last year America was the most generous country on earth meaning that the percentage of US citizens who volunteered and donated money to charity was higher than any other country on earth. Last year (2015) Burma took first (in percentage only) as America's giving went down. According to the *CAF World Giving Index* 61% of Americans gave money and time to charity which is down from 64% the year before. Burma had a score of 66% of its citizens giving proving that the amount you give is not based on how much you make but where your heart is. The average income in Burma is slightly over one fiftieth of the average American income, that is about $1200, yet more Burmese donate money than Americans today. Sadly this trend will continue as long as we keep giving up our morals, pushing out God, and expanding government.

"Do not neglect to show hospitality to strangers, for thereby some have entertained angels unawares."
Hebrews 13:2 (ESV)

America has always been great at showing hospitality and being generous to strangers. This ties in with our value of acceptance, we value what we can do for others and we show that in our generosity. In America we tip generously, we donate generously, we give time generously and we generally value investing in other people.

Most of us fill a need when we see it, we don't wait for the next guy or for the government. For instance let's take a look at some fairly recent natural disasters, Americans donated $1.6 billion after the South Asian tsunami in 2004, $3.3 billion after Hurricane Katrina, and $1.4 billion after the Earthquake in Haiti. That is only what we donated privately if you wanted to count what our government did with tax dollars during these times the number is much greater. We don't sit around and wait for someone else, we give generously to those in need time and time again. In 2014 Americans donated $358 billion dollars which is up 5.4% from 2013. (All numbers from Charity Navigator website)

"Give, and it will be given to you. Good measure, pressed down, shaken together, running over, will be put into your lap. For with the measure you use it will be measured back to you."
Luke 6:38 (ESV)

Most Americans understand that when you aren't willing to put money or effort in, you aren't going to get anything out. This holds true in business, at casinos, in relationships, it holds true everywhere…except government subsidies and Welfare systems. We think it doesn't need to hold true for welfare, we have been disillusioned to think that some things do come for free. This is hurting our generosity, our work ethic, and our motivation. You must give generously to others and your community if you expect them to help you in your time of need. Having said that, don't expect to get something back for giving generously, give with no intention of being repaid, but at the same time never expect to receive without first giving.

We must remember that giving is our duty, and receiving is a privilege. This duty is slipping away fast because of our current entitlement mentality, we assume we should receive before we give when in reality it is the opposite.

FOUNDATION ON GOD'S NATURAL ORDER

America chose to set up a type of government that ruled its people similar to the way God rules nature, in other words natural law. Our founders recognized that we all have natural rights that should be protected. We formed a country around this idea of Gods natural order and by doing so made all men equal and capable to pursue the life that they desire. Sadly it took some time to realize this fully. The Declaration of Independence shows us the three most important natural rights that create a place where we can be individuals on our own journey to the destination of our choice. Let's talk about what these unalienable rights mean for the foundation of our country. What do they make possible and how has that shaped where we are today?

Unalienable Rights given to all men by our creator. America was the first country to truly defend individual rights for all people. By definition a right is sovereign allowing you to act on that right without any permission from others. Our unalienable rights do not require anything from those around us. Unalienable rights cannot be transferred, sold, or surrendered. We have the right to Life, Liberty, and the Pursuit of Happiness. We all have these rights unless we shall do something infringing on another's rights (such as murder) which at that point our rights could be taken away after being proven guilty in a public trial.

These rights provide the basis for the natural order that created our land of prosperity. These unalienable rights are what make the people worthy of being the basis of our government system. Unalienable rights create the basis of real equality by giving everyone the same opportunity. With these rights everyone has the Liberty to pursue their Dreams without government intervention, you don't need to be born to a certain prestige, or have a certain background. These rights are self-evident in nature, and provide a foundation for the individual liberties that create prosperity and joy.

This idea of equality is something that made America different. Other countries such as India and even the U.K. don't fully have our level of equality. Historically the Caste system in India meant that the class you were born into is the class you would always be in. Your role in society was highly defined by your birth. On the other hand the U.K. is very much like we are. It doesn't matter what class you were born into, you do have options to achieve your dreams. Where the U.K. falls short of having the same level of equality is in their government. They are led by a monarch who is determined by birth. In America you can literally be anything you dream, including president, the opportunities are limitless. No racial, generational, or economical circumstance can legally hold you back in America. You always have the opportunity to work hard and create your dreams.

Freedom of Choice was given to all of humanity by God. He does not force you to follow and submit to Him. He does not stop you when you think unwholesome thoughts or prevent you from doing evil things. God permits you to be responsible for yourself and make your own decisions. As an example look at Genesis chapter 3, the fall of man. In Genesis 3 mankind decided to do what the Lord had commanded them not to do, and ate from the tree of knowledge. He did not stop them because He gave them free will and He gives everyone on earth that same right to decide their own destiny.

God does not control us like puppets but rather guides us like a father. He shows His design of the freedom of choice by only the third chapter of the Bible and it continues to be displayed from then till today. God has always given us the choice to follow Him or follow the world. He gives us the responsibility to govern ourselves and our nations. People often deny God's existence because He does not stop evil things from happening, but if you think about that logically, it is impossible to stop all evil things and still allow freedom of choice. In order for Him to eliminate evil we would have to lose our freedom of choice, would you really want that? If so, to what level would you agree with it? Would you give up your power to choose to watch bad movies, get drunk, lie, or cheat? You can't get rid of evil without also getting rid of your individual freedom. That is the same reason our founders created a small and limited government, as government gets bigger free will gets smaller.

Americans strongly value individual freedom and without it America would never have become the great nation it is today. The freedom to make our own decisions is what drives us, without it life loses much of its meaning and joy. Freedom of choice drives individualism and self-worth. When you have free will you are responsible for the outcome. The life you live is a result of your choices, you can choose to make your life meaningful and successful or you can choose to indulge in personal pleasures and selfish desires.

The decision is yours and there are consequences and rewards for each decision, but the bottom line is you are free to make them. America embraced this fundamental principal of freedom and because of that capitalism, freedom of religion, freedom of speech, and individual achievement thrived. Without individual freedom the rights and freedoms that the United States of America is known for would be no more.

Capitalism created an environment which allowed America to grow and flourish quickly. People were not restricted by extensive laws and regulations on business and therefore used their passion and hard work to create wealth and success for themselves. Americans had the idea that you pull your own weight and you provide for yourself. We believed that if you put your mind to it, and work hard enough you can create great wealth for yourself and opportunities for others. Sure enough, we proved that true in our quick rise to the top becoming the biggest economy in the world. In just under one hundred and fifty years after declaring independence America became the richest nation on earth, and I can guarantee that was not due to government control and regulations.

America strongly embraced this idea of freedom in the market place. Your success is up to you, make the right decisions and put your work in the right place and you will reap the rewards. On the other hand becoming lazy and making bad decisions will leave you with the consequences. To put this into an analogy capitalism provides a forest for Americans to either thrive in or fail in. Everyone has access to the same forest, the same trees, the same streams, the same dirt and that provides the same opportunity for everyone to succeed. It all comes down to what decisions you make and how hard you work. You can learn how to become a successful hunter, or you can be the tools the hunter uses to make his hunt successful. The successful hunter hikes around looking for the right place to put bait and he spends hours finding or creating the right tools, such as an accurate gun, a sharp knife, and a truck to get that animal into the freezer. He then employs the skills needed to do the intricate work of shooting, gutting, and processing the hunt. If you decide to be one of the hunter's skills you must be very proficient to carry out one of the tasks the hunter needs accomplished to make the hunt profitable. Capitalism is completely natural in its operation in this way. You can use your skills to control the hunt or use your skills as an employee to carry out the hunt. The key aspect is being successful in a skill that is valuable.

America was able to become the richest nation on earth by a large margin because of the natural idea of capitalism. Even today our country, made up of just 4.4% of the world's population, has a GDP 63% larger than the next richest country, China which makes up roughly 19% of the world's population. Don't forget that before china adopted capitalism the U.S. GDP was 1500% larger. This system of earning your own way to success has paid off greatly. When you are responsible for you own success you work harder, smarter, and more efficiently. Competing with others drives innovation creating fast growing economies, new industries, and new solutions to complicated problems. The flat and free playing field builds large and prosperous economies.

FOUNDATIONAL DOCUMENTS

The Declaration of Independence, the Constitution, and the Bill of Rights are the documents on which American government was built. These documents took the foundational principals we just talked about and create a government that would protect and strengthen them. These documents created a system of government where the people were the focus. That meant keeping the central government small and protecting a land where the people are free to create the kind of life they want to live.

In America you can practice any religion you please, you can participate in free enterprise creating your own business, and if you are elected you can participate in government as well. In America, every citizen has the same rights, which means every person has the same potential, the same playing field under the same rules on which to build their lives. This is why it is called the American Dream, in America everyone can accomplish their dreams if they make the right decisions.

The Declaration of Independence protects the rights that everyone has irrespective of government, and provides the basis of the American idea. It gives the citizens the power to stand against a tyrannical government and defend our rights. The Constitution creates a government congruent with the idea America was built on, it is meant to protect our rights, and defend our country. The Constitution is supposed to be the rule of law that neither the Government nor the Citizen can break. The Bill of

Rights further defines our rights and protects us from losing them to the government. The Bill of Rights is specifically written to protect us from our own government and gives us legal ground to stand on should we have to fight back against a tyrannical government. Without these documents our other foundations could be destroyed by our own government leaving us slaves to a small group of government elites.

The foundation of our country only rests on a few simple things but when those are taken away the whole country will fall to pieces. Our country was built on Biblical and natural principles protected by short and potent founding documents. These worked together in tandem to create a place where liberty can thrive, capitalism can flourish, and dreams can become reality. As we turn away from these corner stones of our country we turn away from our freedom, prosperity, and hope. We cannot let the heritage and foundation of America be trampled by the latest social justice fad, or anti-American idea. We need to stick to our roots and renew these corner stones of our society.

KICK START

- Learn more about America's founding
- Research the beginnings and foundation of some of America's most successful colleges
- Watch Kirk Cameron's *Monumental*
- Visit some American monuments

BROKEN AMERICA

"America's future will be determined by the home and the school. The child becomes largely what he is taught; hence we must watch what we teach, and how we live"
-Jane Addams

Oh boy we've gotten to the part where we talk about what is wrong today. Well the list is long as I'm sure you know but we will just stick to the top four most important problems. The all-encompassing #1 problem is that we have turned away from our heritage and our values. America has lost sight of what it once stood for, we've believed the lies that political correctness and progressivism have told us. The four biggest problems we face in America today are internal. If we fix these problems the economy, foreign policy, discrimination, and oversized government will fix themselves.

We Must Restore

1. Values
2. Education and Media
3. Responsibility
4. Constitutional Government

VALUES

The biggest problem we face in America today is the loss of our True American values. When we hold strong congruent American values the government cannot make decisions the public does not agree with. Also Americans can get along better on a foundation of common values. Here's a refresher on what those core values we need to restore are.

True American Core Values

- Responsibility
- Equality
- Courage
- Independence
- Authenticity
- Honor

Although some Americans still have courage, many have lost it. This is evident in the rise of political correctness and the fall of authenticity. People are losing the courage to say what they believe and stick to it. They are afraid they will be alienated, they're afraid someone will be "offended" and they don't have the courage to be themselves and stand up against public lies on a daily basis. America used to be known as the "Home of the Brave" but these days Americans are addicted to fear and anxiety. We worry about the economy, we worry about our kids' education, we worry about shooters being at school, we worry what people might think of us, we worry about what to say.

What are we the land of the sissies? Are you kidding me? Stop being afraid of life, gain some courage and have a little optimism. Step out and work on solutions for these problems, if you're afraid of your child's education, which is honestly a valid fear with the corruption these days, then do something about it. Home school your kids, find a local homeschool Co-Op they can be a part of, make sure what they are learning is true, and teach them the stuff school is leaving out.

Honestly America needs to grow a back bone, today the home of the brave has turned into the home of the scared and anxious. We must face our fears head on, it works in nature so why can't it work at home? In Africa if you are confronted with a lion you are not supposed to run in fear, the lion knows when you are scared and will surly chase you if you run. Rather you are supposed to face that fear head on, stand your ground, don't let the lion be the stronger one. Act confident and most of the time he will back down.

That doesn't just go for lions either, that is the recommended tactic against almost all animals in the wild. It only takes five seconds of courage to overcome your fear and gain control of the situation. If you can face your fear head on for just five seconds that fear won't grip you so tight and you will be able to accomplish the "impossible." True Americans don't live in fear, they face that fear and find a solution to the problem that caused it.

America also needs to work on individual self-reliance. According to *Pew Research* in 2015, 26% of all young adults 18-34 are living at home. There are some logical reasons like the economy, student debt, ect. But even as they improve the percentage living at home is not decreasing. Self-reliance is fading away, young America has become entitled and many have given up on producing for themselves. When you don't have a job there is government assistance for you, and thanks to Obamacare you can be covered on your parents healthcare till your 26. Yep you heard that right the government just moved its definition of responsible adult up to 26 years old.

Our society keeps perpetuating this idea that we shouldn't grow up. In the 1940s being a teenager as we know it today wasn't a thing, teenagers were expected to work, serve in the military and be ready to support a family of their own. These days it is an excuse for just about anything irresponsible. We have been conditioned that you don't need to "Grow Up" till you're out of college. Many say "I'll only be young once so I might as well do whatever I want." We use our age as an excuse to not grow up and we keep pushing that age range up. Even in the 1960s after the modern idea of the teenager had begun 59% of all 18-29 year olds were married by 2010 it was only 20% according to Pew Research.

This reluctance to "Grow Up" and become responsible is hurting our country politically, economically and ethically. Young professionals and entrepreneurs with a sense of urgency built this country. Ever since the founding of America it is clear that age is not an excuse to forgo responsibility. Today we have roughly one quarter of young adults live in their parent's basement. 240 years ago roughly one quarter of the Declaration signers were what we think of today as young adults, including Thomas

Jefferson the main author who was just 33 at the time. The urgency for action and responsibility is gone when you live with your parents till you're 30. We must revive the value of independence and responsibility to overcome this love of mooching.

Honor and authenticity have also gone missing in American politics, school, media, and big business. We must revive honor and authenticity we need to be trust worthy and act with integrity. Today, Politicians will say one thing to the public while clearly doing the opposite. The problem is that our leaders are representing the public, they aren't the problem, we are. The majority of the American public has lost its honor, its integrity and its responsibility. We need to change ourselves before we can elect honorable leaders that answer to their duty, act responsibly, and have integrity.

SCHOOL AND MAINSTREAM MEDIA

I'm sure some of you are thinking "yeah we really need to fix these" while others are thinking "Uh is this guy nuts? How are these hurting our country?" Well let's look at how public education, college and the mainstream media is destroying our country from the inside out.

First let's talk about the media because it is the more obvious problem. The media has stopped delivering unbiased facts. They pick and choose what information to report depending on their opinion and based on how much money they will make. They constantly bring up stories that downplay a person or group they don't like and quickly breeze over or discount stories that would down play anyone they do like. Much of the mainstream media is on the far left side and it clearly shows through in how they portray different issues and what questions they ask. When interviewing a conservative they always make sure to have a louder liberal there. Then they ask questions from a condemning stance and make the conservative dig their way out of the condemnation. But before they are done the liberal steps in discounting them for something they said before they had time to explain it. They use leading questions to make the answer sound like it supports their argument even when it is saying the opposite.

When they are covering a story they subtly push their agenda in the back-ground. They do this for gun laws, climate change, healthcare, immigration, welfare, basically anything they can find to push their opinion on, they will.

The biggest glaring example of this is when a shooting happens. Every time there is a shooting what does the media say first? "We need more gun laws!" Every time the second amendment is talked about what does the media say? It's out dated and was never intended for the types of guns we have today. The media has this very anti-American idea of guns, virtually every major media outlet supports more gun laws despite less than half of the American public supporting it. They twist the stories of shootings to make it sound like the guns were the problem when in reality the guns would have still been accessible despite more gun laws. The media is the last to admit that the shooter is the actual problem.

Now to the corruption in our school systems. Our public school system has been slowly pushing God and morals out since the early sixties. After God was out of schools they could start teaching moral relativism, basically teaching our kids that there cannot be any absolute moral truth. This puts all moral issues in the realm of opinion, there can be no fact of the matter when it comes to morality, therefore it cannot be true only opinion. This anti-God, Pro Humanism, Pro Socialism turn in our schools has been teaching generations of Americans anti-American views for decades.

Without morality, our form of government cannot stand, the freedom we are to be given in our country only works if people have self-governance which crumbles without morality. When morality is gone, socialism can take root, because it provides a place for these moral relativists to turn to. They can look to the government for their moral decisions and obligations. The government can make the law which then moves to the side of fact because they can prove the law but not morality.

We are seeing the results of this now, every new generation coming out of school is more relativist, more socialist, and more critical of America than the last. It's obvious in how they think. That is why we have more kids living at home longer than ever, one third of our country on some sort of welfare, and the majority of them support the left. They have lost their compass of morality and therefore their drive for the free society America is based on.

After grade school these views are usually backed up and encouraged as most colleges today teach very left wing, anti-God, Big government, politically correct, relativist views as well. They cater to the "minorities" and don't respect other people's viewpoints, even though they claim to be teaching diverse thought and conversation. Freedom of speech is dying faster than ever in college with hate speech codes and know-it-all professors. Some professors are even openly opposing Christianity and threatening bad grades to those who choose to express their faith.

Start Your Search:
Search: Clash between media and ConcernedStudent1950
Search: Professor Fails Faith

Today you pay upwards of $25,000 a year to be told how America is evil, how socialism will fix everything and how the color of your skin determines whether you are privileged or whether "everyone hates you." One worse than that, you pay them to teach you that they can't actually teach you anything in the case of relativism. They forward that truth is relative to what you believe and your perspective, they say there cannot be any absolute truth philosophically. Somehow they convince you that is true by using absolutes to support their argument. If they are forwarding the idea that there are no absolutes, can they really teach you anything? After all they can't teach you what's true, right?

Think about what you believe today, why do you believe it? Is it because of something you learned at school, whether it be grade school or college? Is it something that was suggested you believe? Schools seem to only be teaching and emphasizing the bad parts of American history these days, convincing students that America is evil and greedy. However if you look at both sides a different story emerges, underlining the importance of thinking for yourself based on your own research. Oddly enough the same people pushing the evil America narrative, support the behaviors that created the evil in the first place.

RESPONSIBILITY

Our lack of responsibility, in America today is leading to many different issues: in government, in family life, in business, it affects them all. Responsibility is what makes America work. Without responsibility we cannot have individual liberty, just like misbehaving kids always need a babysitter. It is self-evident that responsibility is something that is absolutely necessary for a thriving society. Sadly, today responsibility is being taught less and less, today many Americans blame others even when it was obviously their fault.

Our government has been so irresponsible with taxpayer money that unless we significantly cut government programs we cannot pay it back. Our government isn't just being irresponsible with our money, its wasting it purposely, our government currently allows illegal aliens to receive welfare, they have been subsidizing and bailing out big companies, and they are continuously adding new welfare and subsidy programs, there is definitely something wrong in terms of responsibility there.

At home we have stopped taking responsibility for our income seeing as now over one third of US citizens are on some sort of welfare. We also don't take responsibility for our kids anymore, we blame society, we blame their friends, and we blame schools when it is up to us to raise our children correctly. With our friends we have started thinking that it was okay to sue over disagreements, we have become quicker to sue than to have a conversation. Our lack of personal responsibility and our love to blame others is ridiculous and if we don't start valuing responsibility soon we won't have anything left to be responsible for.

In business we blame companies for making too much money while we are spending extra to have their product earlier, then we sue them for false advertising when it is clear they were not being serious in their ad. In society we blame CEOs for taking advantage of us as we complain about our 9-5, we insist they just got lucky and became rich. As we're complaining about rich CEOs we are raving about the latest celebrity or the next big movie. Somehow its accepted for movie starts and pop artists to be super rich but it is a crime for CEOs and hedge fund managers.

They all worked very hard to get to the place they are in life so why persecute one but not the other? I think we're mad at the CEOs because we know we could accomplish that if we put in enough work and made the right decisions. When we don't want to put the work in to get there ourselves the next best thing is to take it away from the person that did. These are just a few examples but it should be obvious if you pay attention that we have widely stopped taking responsibility.

CONSTITUTIONAL GOVERNMENT

Whether you realize it or not our government has grown way beyond what the constitution designed it to be. The constitution was meant to give specific power to the federal government. That means the federal government is only meant to have the power talked about in the constitution. Its main jobs are immigration, military, printing money, ensuring fair commerce internationally and between states, and creating any necessary laws for defending the constitution. The bulk of them are listed in article one section eight of the constitution. (Read it in the back) Every power not given to the federal government in the constitution is reserved by the tenth amendment for the states or individuals.

Today our government seems to have flipped that on its head, they are acting as if they have all power except for what is specifically preserved in the bill or rights. Although they have already stepped out of bounds, assuming powers that weren't given to them, they aren't satisfied and further push to revoke rights given to us in the bill of rights such as our freedom of speech and our right to bear arms.

We currently have many laws that are unconstitutional for example the controlled substance act. In the 1920s we recognized that an amendment to the constitution was needed to prohibit alcohol thus came the 18th amendment, later undone by the 21st amendment. So if prohibiting alcohol required an amendment what is different when it comes to the probation on marijuana or any other drug? The federal government cannot constitutionally ban these substances without amending the constitution. Yet our federal government has spent over 1 trillion on the "War on Drugs." Another government action that more openly opposes the constitution is the "Immigration Checkpoints." They openly break the fourth amendment conducting suspicion less and warrantless stops and searches of American citizens.

These checkpoints can be as far as one hundred miles away from the border making it pretty obvious that they are not really questioning your immigration status.

It is the duty of us, the True Americans, to oppose these power grabbing unconstitutional laws, regulations, and actions. We must know our rights and protect them every day, we can't bow down to every government demand, we must only give them the power they are given in the constitution. We are supposed to have a government of, for, and by the people but that cannot last if we the people go along with every unconstitutional and overruling law and regulation the government puts out. We need to stand for our rights, our freedoms and the constitution by which our federal government is meant to be bound.

America is at a turning point right now; we have been lazy not paying attention to our country slipping away around us. We have let our government expand its power to the point where we are losing our individual and constitutional rights. The fork in front of us could take us to new highs and a new age of prosperity or it could destroy everything that ever made America great and strip America of everything that makes it...America.

KICK START

- Pay Attention to the lack of common sense, the ever increasing number of lawsuits, ever increasing regulations, and the contempt for America from some "Americans"
- Take Responsibility
- Think Critically

TURNING POINT

"If destruction be our lot, we must ourselves be its author and finisher. As a nation of freemen, we must live through all time, or die by suicide."
-Abraham Lincoln

America has reached a turning point, if we do not become a new generation of True Americans our country will continue down this path of a slow and painful death. We have the opportunity now to revive freedom, strengthen our rights, and fix our schools but that also leaves the alternative of letting America continue on its path to death. America can once again become the greatest nation on earth if True Americans will step up and become the hardest working, smartest, and most honorable people on earth. Our nation can only be as good as its people so we must wake up, become True Americans and restore this country.

There are two paths before us in 2016 and they both have very different destinations. If we continue on the path we have been on, electing another anti-American like Obama, we will face a very rocky road to mediocrity. If the True Americans rise up, take action, and elect a True American in 2016 we have an opportunity to restore the idea of America and get back on a path toward greatness.

There are two roads in front of us because there are different destinations of the ideology in politics today. There are those who want to fundamentally transform America, their end goal does not include the most significant American values, our unalienable rights to Life, Liberty, and the Pursuit of Happiness. This fundamental change is anti-American and self-evident in America today. On the contrary the True American wants to revive and restore the destination the founders of our country designed. The destination where Life, Liberty, and the Pursuit of Happiness is first and foremost above all, Government is limited, and America is strong. We are at this fork in the road now, we cannot wait, we cannot ignore it. We must revive the True American within ourselves and our country, the time to act is now.

THE WIDE AND EASY ROAD

The road we are on now is the road much traveled. Our country is headed down the path of fundamental change and it is picking up to a sprint. When Obama campaigned he told us what he would do, on October 30, 2008 he said "We are five days away from fundamentally transforming the United States of America" and it is one of the very few things he did not lie about. Today we see the results of that, he has doubled our national debt, weakened our military, created a war on free speech, a war on gun rights, a mandatory purchase of healthcare, and a lack of respect for the law. He is fundamentally changing our country creating a place where some people's rights are trampled and some are given special privileges. He constantly insults the American people, he says they did not build their success, he defends Islam and attacks Christians, and the DHS under his administration says veterans, Christians, and anti-abortionist are likely domestic terrorists. He disrespects our allies and shows no respect for the Constitution. Obama has overstepped his bounds as president and gotten away with it, we cannot let that happen again. If we continue on the road we are on, electing another president like Obama, America will not be American.

If we continue on this path America will face four major consequences that will kill everything America once stood for and possibly the country all together. The four consequences we face should we continue on this wide and easy road are a Financial Death, Loss of our Rights, World government, and Domestic War.

Financial death is easy to picture because it has happened in other countries. Our debt is close to surpassing the level of our GDP, we owe nearly 18 trillion dollars, and our deficit is a little under half a trillion dollars, the lowest it's been since 2007 when it was just 161 billion. With the deficit being at about half a trillion dollars that means that we add a trillion dollars to our debt every other year at current spending levels. We currently have no solution to pay it off besides higher taxes. We are already at a point where if we paid off $350,000 a minute it would take 100 years to pay off our debt, and that's assuming our deficit is zero. Raising taxes to pay off our debt won't get us out of it either because it stunts economic growth.

Not only is our country irresponsible but we have also been teaching younger generations to live for the moment and not think about the future. College students are borrowing astronomical amounts of money for degrees that don't have jobs and the result is 1.2 trillion dollars of government loans to students that can't pay them back. We are creating a generation dependent on welfare and slaves to student loans. We are already slaves to tax debt that we don't currently have a way out of. We have been taking free handouts from government and getting degrees that won't earn us money, then voting for the people who created that problem because they will give us more free stuff.

We are already slaves to decades of paying for debt we didn't sign up for but we are choosing to sign up for even more, so much more that it will be deadly if we continue. If we continue on this route for another presidency our debt and lack of a solution to pay it down will crumble our economy, people will stop investing in us, and not only will our economy crash, as we saw from the 2008 recession, when we go down, the rest of the world goes down as well.

To fix this problem we need to reduce government and its spending levels. We need to reduce government regulation creating a more free market to grow our economy, we need to reduce welfare, social security, and government health plans and we need to get people back to work. Ongoing and unnecessary foreign aid needs to be reduced or stopped. Most of all our government has to stop spending money that it doesn't have, rather than going into debt and raising taxes to justify their spending.

It is our job to get our government in check, we

need a less intrusive government for a healthier and faster growing economy and we need a responsible government that doesn't spend our money on inefficient or useless things especially when it is money we do not have yet. We must make our government responsible because we are the ones saddled with the debt and if we are irresponsible with our economy we risk hurting billions of others around the world.

Loss of our Rights, this one has also already begun. We can see this in the fight against our first amendment rights with the loss of the right to deny service based on religious convictions, and hate speech codes on college campuses.

Freedom of speech is not gone, but it is very suppressed by the political correctness being pushed by our news and the left. Over time the majority of America has been tricked into thinking that free speech is bad because your views might be offensive to someone. Freedom of speech is what made us such a responsible people in the first place, when someone was out of line we called them out on it, these days when you do that your called a bigot, a racist, ignorant, or evil. As freedom of speech dies we lose the ability to be a country "For the people, Of the people and By the people".

America has fallen far into the trap of political correctness and as we fall further into that trap we lose more and more of our rights. Political correctness continuously hides the truth and allows the niceties of lies to prevail, if we don't stop sweeping things under the rug like the media and our government has been doing we will later realize we've built a mountain.

Their opposition to our Second Amendment rights is also stronger and stronger as Obama's presidency comes to an end. Further still we have lost our fifth and sixth amendment rights to the 2012 NDAA and fourth amendment to warrantless searches at inland border checkpoints. We allow the right to life to be taken away from hundreds of thousands of babies a year through abortion. Our government has no intention of protecting our right in fact our government has been doing the opposite for quite some time. Recently our rights have been fading very quickly and if we continue down the path Obama has been taking us we will lose them all.

One world government sounds like conspiracy but when you think about it, it seems to be happening already. Our leaders are working toward a one world governing force, the U.N. agenda 21 recently replaced by the 2030 agenda is a perfect example of the push for one world government and if realized will strip America of all its freedoms. The 2030 Agenda aims to completely end poverty and hunger, protect the planet from climate change, ensure that all humans prosper in harmony with nature, and have world peace. Sure that might all sound good in theory but when you start thinking about what is needed to accomplish that a new story emerges.

What could a government do to end world poverty? Wealth redistribution via centralized federally controlled banks. How do they protect the planet from climate change? Insane taxes, as well as limits on food, distance traveled, private business, and private property. World peace, of course the most unrealistic one, to accomplish this they will limit just about every individual freedom you have, they would create a place similar to that in the Hunger Game and Divergent movies.

The leadership of the U.S. has been onboard with plans such as the 2030 agenda and will continue to be if we continue on the path of Obama. We have not had True American leadership in the white house for decades and if we continue to elect people who do not reduce government uphold the constitution and fight for freedom our country will cease to be. The U.S.A. was built on the idea of freedom for its people but we have let the government grow taking away our power and worse giving it the ability to give away its own power to further world government agendas such as those created by the world's highest leaders behind the closed doors of the U.N.

We must get off of this path because the more powerful government gets the less freedom we have and the more of a threat it is to the citizenry. History has proven time and time again that big government especially authoritarian and totalitarian style governments are among the biggest threats to human life. The 21st century is regarded as the bloodiest century in history due to large overruling governments putting too much power in the hands of a few. These governments and their cold blooded leaders killed tens of millions of people and started bloody wars for political and ideological reasons proving the point that large government is a great threat to its citizens.

According to R.J. Rummel in his book *Death by Government* there has been over 169 million murdered by government since 1900, he calls this Democide which encompasses genocide, politicide, and mass murder. The top three deadliest countries account for 68% of all the killed. The USSR killed about 61 million, China (PRC) around 35 million, and Nazi Germany in the ball park of 20 million. These numbers are so high it's hard to imagine they are actual deaths, but no matter how you look at it we are talking about tens of millions of civilians murdered by big government. The elite in power of overreaching and over controlling governments have time and again proven that power corrupts.

Americas founders realized this and created and advocated for a small, limited, and balanced central government. We have already given to much power to our federal government, if the worlds governments band together to create a world government all hope for freedom is lost. The bigger we let government grow the greater risk we put ourselves in not only of losing our rights but also our lives.

War in foreign lands is inevitable at this point. We have turned a blind eye to Iran's intentions to destroy Israel and the U.S. as well as let ISIS grow far too large. If we continue with the weak foreign policy of the left we will see war on home turf. Another presidency of allowing non-trustworthy countries like Iran to have access to billions of dollars and continue nuclear development will result in war both foreign and at home. Iran chants "Death to America" "Death to Great Britain" and "Death to Israel" at major political events talking about the Iran nuclear deal Obama made with them.

The Obama administration has been sympathetic to countries that were previously enemies and are openly against America and her greatest allies. It sounds unimaginable to most Americans but If we continue our weak foreign policy we will face war in our back yard. Sadly North Korea, Russia, Iran, and ISIS are not all we face if we have another liberal or republican in name only presidency.

There is already an ideological war between the Liberals and Conservatives because of the different destinations each party wants for America. If the liberals win another presidency and continue to attack our constitutional rights there will be a civil war between the True Americans and those who advocate a government similar to those of Europe. There would be a civil war for the constitution against those who seek to "Fundamentally transform" the American idea, her rights, and her heritage.

Our current path leads to destruction, we must stand up and take action against this path we are on and elect a True American who will adhere to the principles and values of the constitution.

THE NARROW AND EXCEPTIONAL PATH

This is the path that our founders took, not only did they take it but they created it. When they started this country on the idea of freedom, equality, the rule of law, and limited government it was something that had never been done before. They created a better path for a nation and a better way to live life that is now being copied in part by people all around the world. So how can we get back to this path and the sustainable rewards it leads to? To get back to this path we the people of the United States of America need to become True Americans. We need to understand the founding of America, understand the purpose, ideas, and principles behind that founding, and we need to uphold the documents that our founders wrote to safeguard us from ourselves and big government. If we as a people stand up teach, what our schools have twisted or left out and truly stand for the purpose, ideas, and principles that created this country we can make it great once again.

What does the future hold if we get back to the constitution and the principles it was meant to protect? A constitutional future will first of all release us from the massive pile of laws and regulations that currently restrict our freedom and make us subjects of our government. Secondly, it will once again make us the "City on a Hill" that the rest of the world can look to when shaping their governments and their lives. Third it will revive the American dream, under a small constitutional government you will be free to express yourself and your business the way you want, once again creating more opportunity and more autonomy. Forth under a constitutional limited government the Feds can get back to what they were designed for and protect our country from outside forces such as the problems in the middle east and halting the crazy U.N. Agendas.

The Federal government was never intended to control education, insurance, drugs, bailouts, or wealth redistribution. The federal governments job is to protect America and her rights for any and all who should try to take them. The Federal government is literally supposed to stop organizations like our federal government. We the people, the True Americans must stand up and take action against the current direction of our government. We must defend the Constitution and the principals it stands for. If we don't America will die, and its greatness will be lost.

KICK START

- Watch and/or read the *Atlas Shrugged* series to see the full picture of what it looks like when government over-regulates the economy.
- Spread the news about the decision America has before it

AMERICA NEEDS YOU

*"The tree of liberty must be refreshed from time to time
with the blood of patriots and tyrants"*
-Thomas Jefferson

True Americans are needed for the survival of America. Without America the hope of true freedom and unlimited dreams is lost. It is our duty to take responsibility for our country and the future of everyone around us. We must become True Americans, we must hold true to the idea of America. We cannot let America follow the path of every other country on earth, we must defend what makes us unique. We must learn our real heritage and stick to it. It is our job to defend the constitution and the philosophies and ideals within. If we don't defend the constitution to protect our freedoms and the power of the people we will lose the country we know and love. It is time to step up, take action, and be a True American.

A True American takes Full Responsibility. They are honest and sincere about who they are. Honorable in their actions, their attitude, and their courage. Every True American must have a strong set of values that is congruent with Gods ethics and the founding fathers vision of a free land. True Americans are willing to risk it all for freedom and they never surrender their rights. It is time for us to be these people once again.

True Americans built this country with their own hands. They came from all different walks of life yet they put that behind them and looked to a brighter future, one that they would build and many generations to come would enjoy. We are living in the result of the freedom that countless lives were sacrificed for. We are living in the land of opportunity because True Americans worked tirelessly to secure it. We are enjoying the fruit of those courageous True Americans. But we are letting it die, we are letting social justice worriers and anti-American leftists destroy everything our ancestors and our soldiers died to protect. We are taking this amazing gift for granted and throwing it out as if it were a candy wrapper.

How can we let our ancestors die in vain? How can we let the freedom so many fought for be taken away willingly? How can we let government, historically the largest mass murdering tool in all of creation, grow so large and powerful? Why are we falling into their trap to steal our freedom? How long will we let our governments power go unchecked?

Our founding fathers created a republic because they knew that the majority of people would sway in the wind following the whims of political hype. They were right, but the one thing their system could not account for is when the majority of those in power create the political hype to justify striping the people of their rights. We need to see through the hype, and recognize when they are using it to take our rights. In just the last two decades they have used 9/11 to justify the Patriot act which took away our fourth amendment right to privacy and fifth amendment right to a fair trial. Currently they are using equality and diversity to take away our first amendments right to free speech. They constantly employ mass shootings to justify taking our second amendment right to bear arms. Let's not forget terrorism to expand NSA surveillance.

Events such as these are horrible and there should be measures taken to defend against them but those measures should not include the loss of our rights or the expansion of government. Our founding fathers knew what horrible injustices would be done but they knew large government was not the answer. Our founding fathers fought a great war to escape from a large over ruling government that was a threat to the people.

Today our government has slyly fed us lies through assumptions, they have tricked us in to believing that they are needed for the safety, riches, and wellbeing of the people, and we have bought their lie and allowed them to grow. Because we have let our government transform from servings and protecting the people's rights, to making the people subject to it we have created the very thing our ancestors fought and died to break away from. Benjamin Franklin called out those who sacrifice their values and their rights for safety and prosperity in the *Poor Richards Almanack*. He said:

> *"Sell not virtue to purchase wealth,*
> *nor Liberty to purchase power"*

Benjamin Franklin used a similar phrase when

negotiating with Great Britain in 1775 before the Revolutionary War. He said:

"They who can give up essential liberty to obtain a little temporary safety, deserve neither liberty nor safety."

Our founding fathers valued liberty above all else. The government we have currently would be appalling to them because it is just as controlling as the government they sought freedom from. We have given up far too much liberty for a false sense of safety. We have put far too much power in the hands of Washington making them a threat to the American people as well as potentially the world. We have given them power to monitor our lives in the name of "stopping terrorism" but they use it instead to monitor and shut down those who speak against them. We allow them to have internal "Immigration checkpoints" yet they give welfare benefits and sanctuary to illegal aliens. We allow them to push gun control even after they allow "gun walking" to Mexican drug cartels. ("Gun walking" is deliberately allowing guns to land in the hands of criminals) They got away with Obamacare despite over half of the United States citizens opposition which lead to lawsuits from 27 states questioning its constitutionality.

Every time government takes on a new task its power over us grows. For instance government has created a guaranteed method of control over us with welfare and our growing dependence on it. Most of us would never actually vote to stop federal social welfare programs and as long as they have that excuse to continue to raise tax revenue they can continue to raise spending on other areas we may not even know about. Since we have started continual federal taxation and welfare our government has only grown. Due to the flaws in our welfare program it produces a class of people that will always vote for those who seek to expand government, and thus the problem arises. The more money, and control we submit to the government, the more they will ask for and take, we can't keep rolling over to their demands. It is time to take back liberty and regain our countries virtue.

It is no longer enough to fight for freedom only in the voting booth. We need to fight for freedom at school, we need to defend it in our homes, we need to defend it on social media, we must revive our freedom. It's not enough to just act like a True American, it's not enough to read this book and share it, we need to become and create True Americans. We need to correct our culture before it is too late.

The only way we can return to the freedom and prosperity of our past is if we change the mindset and ideals of our culture. If we continue to allow the mindset of entitlement and the excuse of blame we will never return to a great America. The longer we allow ourselves and our friends to be uninformed about our countries past and where it is today the harder it will be to recover. It's time for a revival of the American spirit and a renewing of America's real Judeo-Christian heritage. It is time to stand up against those who oppose the founding and the principles of America.

If you have known that America was slipping away but haven't done anything about it now is the time. If you want a free land for your kids and the generations to come you must act now. If your serious about your love for America, you've got to get off the couch. We have been too soft for too long and now is the time strengthen our minds and begin the revival, and renewal of America. The time is now, we must, **Dare To Be American.**

Thank You for reading this book, now that you have an idea of what is going on please make the commitment, today, to continue to take responsibility for your country, go to daretobeamerican.com/commit/ to actualize this in your mind and continue to learn about living with a True American mindset. Please help further these ideas by writing a review and sharing with your friends.

FOUNDING DOCUMENT

TRANSCRIPTS

DECLARATION OF INDEPENDENCE

IN CONGRESS, JULY 4, 1776.

The unanimous Declaration of the thirteen united States of America,

When in the Course of human events, it becomes necessary for one people to dissolve the political bands which have connected them with another, and to assume among the powers of the earth, the separate and equal station to which the Laws of Nature and of Nature's God entitle them, a decent respect to the opinions of mankind requires that they should declare the causes which impel them to the separation.

We hold these truths to be self-evident, that all men are created equal, that they are endowed by their Creator with certain unalienable Rights, that among these are Life, Liberty and the pursuit of Happiness.--That to secure these rights, Governments are instituted among Men, deriving their just powers from the consent of the governed, --That whenever any Form of Government becomes destructive of these ends, it is the Right of the People to alter or to abolish it, and to institute new Government, laying its foundation on such principles and organizing its powers in such form, as to them shall seem most likely to effect their Safety and Happiness. Prudence, indeed, will dictate that Governments long established should not be changed for light and transient causes; and accordingly all experience hath shewn, that mankind are more disposed to suffer, while evils are sufferable, than to right themselves by abolishing the forms to which they are accustomed. But when a long train of abuses and usurpations, pursuing invariably the same Object evinces a design to reduce them under absolute Despotism, it is their right, it is their duty, to throw off such Government, and to provide new Guards for their future security.--Such has been the patient sufferance of these Colonies; and such is now the necessity which constrains them to alter their former Systems of Government. The history of the present King of Great Britain is a history of repeated injuries and usurpations, all having in direct object the establishment of an absolute Tyranny over these States. To prove this, let Facts be submitted to a candid world.

He has refused his Assent to Laws, the most wholesome and necessary for the public good.

He has forbidden his Governors to pass Laws of immediate and pressing importance, unless suspended in their operation till his Assent should be obtained; and when so suspended, he has utterly neglected to attend to them.

He has refused to pass other Laws for the accommodation of large districts of people, unless those people would relinquish the right of Representation in the Legislature, a right inestimable to them and formidable to tyrants only.

He has called together legislative bodies at places unusual, uncomfortable, and distant from the depository of their public Records, for the sole purpose of fatiguing them into compliance with his measures.

He has dissolved Representative Houses repeatedly, for opposing with manly firmness his invasions on the rights of the people.

He has refused for a long time, after such dissolutions, to cause others to be elected; whereby the Legislative powers, incapable of Annihilation, have returned to the People at large for their exercise; the State remaining in the mean time exposed to all the dangers of invasion from without, and convulsions within.

He has endeavoured to prevent the population of these States; for that purpose obstructing the Laws for Naturalization of Foreigners; refusing to pass others to encourage their migrations hither, and raising the conditions of new Appropriations of Lands.

He has obstructed the Administration of Justice, by refusing his Assent to Laws for establishing Judiciary powers.

He has made Judges dependent on his Will alone, for the tenure of their offices, and the amount and payment of their salaries.

He has erected a multitude of New Offices, and sent hither swarms of Officers to harrass our people, and eat out their substance.

He has kept among us, in times of peace, Standing Armies without the Consent of our legislatures.

He has affected to render the Military independent of and superior to the Civil power.

He has combined with others to subject us to a jurisdiction foreign to our constitution, and unacknowledged by our laws; giving his Assent to their Acts of pretended Legislation:

For Quartering large bodies of armed troops among us:

For protecting them, by a mock Trial, from punishment for any Murders which they should commit on the Inhabitants of these States:

For cutting off our Trade with all parts of the world:

For imposing Taxes on us without our Consent:

For depriving us in many cases, of the benefits of Trial by Jury:

For transporting us beyond Seas to be tried for pretended offences

For abolishing the free System of English Laws in a neighbouring Province, establishing therein an Arbitrary government, and enlarging its Boundaries so as to render it at once an example and fit instrument for introducing the same absolute rule into these Colonies:

For taking away our Charters, abolishing our most valuable Laws, and altering fundamentally the Forms of our Governments:

For suspending our own Legislatures, and declaring themselves invested with power to legislate for us in all cases whatsoever.

He has abdicated Government here, by declaring us out of his Protection and waging War against us.

He has plundered our seas, ravaged our Coasts, burnt our towns, and destroyed the lives of our people.

He is at this time transporting large Armies of foreign Mercenaries to compleat the works of death, desolation and tyranny, already begun with circumstances of Cruelty & perfidy scarcely paralleled in the most barbarous ages, and totally unworthy the Head of a civilized nation.

He has constrained our fellow Citizens taken Captive on the high Seas to bear Arms against their Country, to become the executioners of their friends and Brethren, or to fall themselves by their Hands.

He has excited domestic insurrections amongst us, and has endeavoured to bring on the inhabitants of our frontiers, the merciless Indian Savages, whose known rule of warfare, is an undistinguished destruction of all ages, sexes and conditions.

In every stage of these Oppressions We have Petitioned for Redress in the most humble terms: Our repeated Petitions have been answered only by repeated injury. A Prince whose character is thus marked by every act which may define a Tyrant, is unfit to be the ruler of a free people.

Nor have We been wanting in attentions to our Brittish brethren. We have warned them from time to time of attempts by their legislature to extend an unwarrantable jurisdiction over us. We have reminded them of the circumstances of our emigration and settlement here. We have appealed to their native justice and magnanimity, and we have conjured them by the ties of our common kindred to disavow these usurpations, which, would inevitably interrupt our connections and correspondence. They too have been deaf to the voice of justice and of consanguinity. We must, therefore, acquiesce in the necessity, which denounces our Separation, and hold them, as we hold the rest of mankind, Enemies in War, in Peace Friends.

We, therefore, the Representatives of the united States of America, in General Congress, Assembled, appealing to the Supreme Judge of the world for the rectitude of our intentions, do, in the Name, and by Authority of the good People of these Colonies, solemnly publish and declare, That these United Colonies are, and of Right ought to be Free and Independent States; that they are Absolved from all Allegiance to the British Crown, and that all political connection between them and the State of Great Britain, is and ought to be totally dissolved; and that as Free and Independent States, they have full Power to levy War, conclude Peace, contract Alliances, establish Commerce, and to do all other Acts and Things which Independent States may of right do. And for the support of this Declaration, with a firm reliance on the protection of divine Providence, we mutually pledge to each other our Lives, our Fortunes and our sacred Honor.

SIGNERS

Georgia	Button Gwinnett
	Lyman Hall
	George Walton
North Carolina	William Hooper
	Joseph Hewes
	John Penn
South Carolina	Edward Rutledge
	Thomas Heyward, Jr.
	Thomas Lynch, Jr.
	Arthur Middleton
Massachusetts	John Hancock
	Samuel Adams
	John Adams
	Robert Treat Paine

	Elbridge Gerry
Maryland	Samuel Chase
	William Paca
	Thomas Stone
	Charles Carroll of Carrollton
Virginia	George Wythe
	Richard Henry Lee
	Thomas Jefferson
	Benjamin Harrison
	Thomas Nelson, Jr.
	Francis Lightfoot Lee
	Carter Braxton
Pennsylvania	Robert Morris
	Benjamin Rush
	Benjamin Franklin
	John Morton
	George Clymer
	James Smith
	George Taylor
	James Wilson
	George Ross
Delaware	Caesar Rodney
	George Read
	Thomas McKean
New York	William Floyd
	Philip Livingston
	Francis Lewis
	Lewis Morris
New Jersey	Richard Stockton
	John Witherspoon
	Francis Hopkinson
	John Hart
	Abraham Clark
New Hampshire	Josiah Bartlett
	William Whipple
	Matthew Thornton
Rhode Island	Stephen Hopkins
	William Ellery
Connecticut	Roger Sherman
	Samuel Huntington
	William Williams
	Oliver Wolcott

CONSTITUTION

All passages in brackets "[ ]" will have the number of the amendment that changed them directly after it, e.g. "(15th)"

We the People of the United States, in Order to form a more perfect Union, establish Justice, insure domestic Tranquility, provide for the common defence, promote the general Welfare, and secure the Blessings of Liberty to ourselves and our Posterity, do ordain and establish this Constitution for the United States of America.

ARTICLE. I.

Section. 1.

All legislative Powers herein granted shall be vested in a Congress of the United States, which shall consist of a Senate and House of Representatives.

Section. 2.

The House of Representatives shall be composed of Members chosen every second Year by the People of the several States, and the Electors in each State shall have the Qualifications requisite for Electors of the most numerous Branch of the State Legislature.

No Person shall be a Representative who shall not have attained to the Age of twenty five Years, and been seven Years a Citizen of the United States, and who shall not, when elected, be an Inhabitant of that State in which he shall be chosen.

[Representatives and direct Taxes shall be apportioned among the several States which may be included within this Union, according to their respective Numbers, which shall be determined by adding to the whole Number of free Persons, including those bound to Service for a Term of Years, and excluding Indians not taxed, three fifths of all other Persons.] (14th) The actual Enumeration shall be made within three Years after the first Meeting of the Congress of the United States, and within every subsequent Term of ten Years, in such Manner as they shall by Law direct. The Number of Representatives shall not exceed one for every thirty Thousand, but each State shall have at Least one Representative; and until such enumeration shall be made, the State of New Hampshire shall be entitled to chuse three, Massachusetts eight, Rhode-Island and Providence Plantations one, Connecticut five, New-York six, New Jersey four, Pennsylvania eight, Delaware one, Maryland six, Virginia ten, North Carolina five, South Carolina five, and Georgia three.

When vacancies happen in the Representation from any State, the Executive Authority thereof shall issue Writs of Election to fill such Vacancies.

The House of Representatives shall chuse their Speaker and other Officers; and shall have the sole Power of Impeachment.

Section. 3.

The Senate of the United States shall be composed of two Senators from each State, [chosen by the Legislature thereof,] (17th) for six Years; and each Senator shall have one Vote.

Immediately after they shall be assembled in Consequence of the first Election, they shall be divided as equally as may be into three Classes. The Seats of the Senators of the first Class shall be vacated at the Expiration of the second Year, of the second Class at the Expiration of the fourth Year, and of the third Class at the Expiration of the sixth Year, so that one third may be chosen every second Year; [and if Vacancies happen by Resignation, or otherwise, during the Recess of the Legislature of any State, the Executive thereof may make temporary Appointments until the next Meeting of the Legislature, which shall then fill such Vacancies.] (17th)

No Person shall be a Senator who shall not have attained to the Age of thirty Years, and been nine Years a Citizen of the United States, and who shall not, when elected, be an Inhabitant of that State for which he shall be chosen.

The Vice President of the United States shall be President of the Senate, but shall have no Vote, unless they be equally divided.

The Senate shall chuse their other Officers, and also a President pro tempore, in the Absence of the Vice President, or when he shall exercise the Office of President of the United States.

The Senate shall have the sole Power to try all Impeachments. When sitting for that Purpose, they shall be on Oath or Affirmation. When the President of the United States is tried, the Chief Justice shall preside: And no Person shall be convicted without the Concurrence of two thirds of the Members present.

Judgment in Cases of Impeachment shall not extend further than to removal from Office, and disqualification to hold and enjoy any Office of honor, Trust or Profit under the United States: but the Party convicted shall nevertheless be liable and subject to Indictment, Trial, Judgment and Punishment, according to Law.

Section. 4.

The Times, Places and Manner of holding Elections for Senators and Representatives, shall be prescribed in each State by the Legislature thereof; but the Congress may at any time by Law make or alter such Regulations, except as to the Places of chusing Senators.

The Congress shall assemble at least once in every Year, and such Meeting shall be [on the first Monday in December,] (20th) unless they shall by Law appoint a different Day.

Section. 5.

Each House shall be the Judge of the Elections, Returns and Qualifications of its own Members, and a Majority of each shall constitute a Quorum to do Business; but a smaller Number may adjourn from day to day, and may be authorized to compel the Attendance of absent Members, in such Manner, and under such Penalties as each House may provide.

Each House may determine the Rules of its Proceedings, punish its Members for disorderly Behaviour, and, with the Concurrence of two thirds, expel a Member.

Each House shall keep a Journal of its Proceedings, and from time to time publish the same, excepting such Parts as may in their Judgment require Secrecy; and the Yeas and Nays of the Members of either House on any question shall, at the Desire of one fifth of those Present, be entered on the Journal.

Neither House, during the Session of Congress, shall, without the Consent of the other, adjourn for more than three days, nor to any other Place than that in which the two Houses shall be sitting.

Section. 6.

The Senators and Representatives shall receive a Compensation for their Services, to be ascertained by Law, and paid out of the Treasury of the United States. They shall in all Cases, except Treason, Felony and Breach of the Peace, be privileged from Arrest during their Attendance at the Session of their respective Houses, and in going to and returning from the same; and for any Speech or Debate in either House, they shall not be questioned in any other Place.

No Senator or Representative shall, during the Time for which he was elected, be appointed to any civil Office under the Authority of the United States, which shall have been created, or the Emoluments whereof shall have been encreased during such time; and no Person holding any Office under the United States, shall be a Member of either House during his Continuance in Office.

Section. 7.

All Bills for raising Revenue shall originate in the House of Representatives; but the Senate may propose or concur with Amendments as on other Bills.

Every Bill which shall have passed the House of Representatives and the Senate, shall, before it become a Law, be presented to the President of the United States; If he approve he shall sign it, but if not he shall return it, with his Objections to that House in which it shall have originated, who shall enter the Objections at large on their Journal, and proceed to reconsider it. If after such Reconsideration two thirds of that House shall agree to pass the Bill, it shall be sent, together with the Objections, to the other House, by which it shall likewise be reconsidered, and if approved by two thirds of that House, it shall become a Law. But in all such Cases the Votes of both Houses shall be determined by yeas and Nays, and the Names of the Persons voting for and against the Bill shall be entered on the Journal of each House respectively. If any Bill shall not be returned by the President within ten Days (Sundays excepted) after it shall have been presented to him, the

Same shall be a Law, in like Manner as if he had signed it, unless the Congress by their Adjournment prevent its Return, in which Case it shall not be a Law.

Every Order, Resolution, or Vote to which the Concurrence of the Senate and House of Representatives may be necessary (except on a question of Adjournment) shall be presented to the President of the United States; and before the Same shall take Effect, shall be approved by him, or being disapproved by him, shall be repassed by two thirds of the Senate and House of Representatives, according to the Rules and Limitations prescribed in the Case of a Bill.

Section. 8.

The Congress shall have Power To lay and collect Taxes, Duties, Imposts and Excises, to pay the Debts and provide for the common Defence and general Welfare of the United States; but all Duties, Imposts and Excises shall be uniform throughout the United States;

To borrow Money on the credit of the United States;

To regulate Commerce with foreign Nations, and among the several States, and with the Indian Tribes;

To establish an uniform Rule of Naturalization, and uniform Laws on the subject of Bankruptcies throughout the United States;

To coin Money, regulate the Value thereof, and of foreign Coin, and fix the Standard of Weights and Measures;

To provide for the Punishment of counterfeiting the Securities and current Coin of the United States;

To establish Post Offices and post Roads;

To promote the Progress of Science and useful Arts, by securing for limited Times to Authors and Inventors the exclusive Right to their respective Writings and Discoveries;

To constitute Tribunals inferior to the supreme Court;

To define and punish Piracies and Felonies committed on the high Seas, and Offences against the Law of Nations;

To declare War, grant Letters of Marque and Reprisal, and make Rules concerning Captures on Land and Water;

To raise and support Armies, but no Appropriation of Money to that Use shall be for a longer Term than two Years;

To provide and maintain a Navy;

To make Rules for the Government and Regulation of the land and naval Forces;

To provide for calling forth the Militia to execute the Laws of the Union, suppress Insurrections and repel Invasions;

To provide for organizing, arming, and disciplining, the Militia, and for governing such Part of them as may be employed in the Service of the United States, reserving to the States respectively, the Appointment of the Officers, and the Authority of training the Militia according to the discipline prescribed by Congress;

To exercise exclusive Legislation in all Cases whatsoever, over such District (not exceeding ten Miles square) as may, by Cession of particular States, and the Acceptance of Congress, become the Seat of the Government of the United States, and to exercise like Authority over all Places purchased by the Consent of the Legislature of the State in which the Same shall be, for the Erection of Forts, Magazines, Arsenals, dock-Yards, and other needful Buildings;—And

To make all Laws which shall be necessary and proper for carrying into Execution the foregoing Powers, and all other Powers vested by this Constitution in the Government of the United States, or in any Department or Officer thereof.

Section. 9.

The Migration or Importation of such Persons as any of the States now existing shall think proper to admit, shall not be prohibited by the Congress prior to the Year one thousand eight hundred and eight, but a Tax or duty may be imposed on such Importation, not exceeding ten dollars for each Person.

The Privilege of the Writ of Habeas Corpus shall not be suspended, unless when in Cases of Rebellion or Invasion the public Safety may require it.

No Bill of Attainder or ex post facto Law shall be passed.

No Capitation, or other direct, Tax shall be laid, [unless in Proportion to the Census or enumeration herein before directed to be taken.] (16th)

No Tax or Duty shall be laid on Articles exported from any State.

No Preference shall be given by any Regulation of Commerce or Revenue to the Ports of one State over those of another: nor shall Vessels bound to, or from, one State, be obliged to enter, clear, or pay Duties in another.

No Money shall be drawn from the Treasury, but in Consequence of Appropriations made by Law; and a regular Statement and Account of the Receipts and Expenditures of all public Money shall be published from time to time.

No Title of Nobility shall be granted by the United States: And no Person holding any Office of Profit or Trust under them, shall, without the Consent of the Congress, accept of any present, Emolument, Office, or Title, of any kind whatever, from any King, Prince, or foreign State.

Section. 10.

No State shall enter into any Treaty, Alliance, or Confederation; grant Letters of Marque and Reprisal; coin Money; emit Bills of Credit; make any Thing but gold and silver Coin a Tender in Payment of Debts; pass any Bill of Attainder, ex post facto Law, or Law impairing the Obligation of Contracts, or grant any Title of Nobility.

No State shall, without the Consent of the Congress, lay any Imposts or Duties on Imports or Exports, except what may be absolutely necessary for executing it's inspection Laws: and the net Produce of all Duties and Imposts, laid by any State on Imports or Exports, shall be for the Use of the Treasury of the United States; and all such Laws shall be subject to the Revision and Controul of the Congress.

No State shall, without the Consent of Congress, lay any Duty of Tonnage, keep Troops, or Ships of War in time of Peace, enter into any Agreement or Compact with another State, or with a foreign Power, or engage in War, unless actually invaded, or in such imminent Danger as will not admit of delay.

ARTICLE. II.

Section. 1.

The executive Power shall be vested in a President of the United States of America. He shall hold his Office during the Term of four Years, and, together with the Vice President, chosen for the same Term, be elected, as follows

Each State shall appoint, in such Manner as the Legislature thereof may direct, a Number of Electors, equal to the whole Number of Senators and Representatives to which the State may be entitled in the Congress: but no Senator or Representative, or Person holding an Office of Trust or Profit under the United States, shall be appointed an Elector.

[The Electors shall meet in their respective States, and vote by Ballot for two Persons, of whom one at least shall not be an Inhabitant of the same State with themselves. And they shall make a List of all the Persons voted for, and of the Number of Votes for each; which List they shall sign and certify, and transmit sealed to the Seat of the Government of the United States, directed to the President of the Senate. The President of the Senate shall, in the Presence of the Senate and House of Representatives, open all the Certificates, and the Votes shall then be counted. The Person having the greatest Number of Votes shall be the President, if such Number be a Majority of the whole Number of Electors appointed; and if there be more than one who have such Majority, and have an equal Number of Votes, then the House of Representatives shall immediately chuse by Ballot one of them for President; and if no Person have a Majority, then from the five highest on the List the said House shall in like Manner chuse the President. But in chusing the President, the Votes shall be taken by States, the Representation from each State having one Vote; A quorum for this Purpose shall consist of a Member or Members from two thirds of the States, and a Majority of all the States shall be necessary to a Choice. In every Case, after the Choice of the President, the Person having the greatest Number of Votes of the Electors shall be the Vice President. But if there should remain two or more who have equal Votes, the

Senate shall chuse from them by Ballot the Vice President.] (12ᵗʰ)

The Congress may determine the Time of chusing the Electors, and the Day on which they shall give their Votes; which Day shall be the same throughout the United States.

No Person except a natural born Citizen, or a Citizen of the United States, at the time of the Adoption of this Constitution, shall be eligible to the Office of President; neither shall any Person be eligible to that Office who shall not have attained to the Age of thirty five Years, and been fourteen Years a Resident within the United States.

[In Case of the Removal of the President from Office, or of his Death, Resignation, or Inability to discharge the Powers and Duties of the said Office, the Same shall devolve on the Vice President, and the Congress may by Law provide for the Case of Removal, Death, Resignation or Inability, both of the President and Vice President, declaring what Officer shall then act as President, and such Officer shall act accordingly, until the Disability be removed, or a President shall be elected.] (25ᵗʰ)

The President shall, at stated Times, receive for his Services, a Compensation, which shall neither be encreased nor diminished during the Period for which he shall have been elected, and he shall not receive within that Period any other Emolument from the United States, or any of them.

Before he enter on the Execution of his Office, he shall take the following Oath or Affirmation:—"I do solemnly swear (or affirm) that I will faithfully execute the Office of President of the United States, and will to the best of my Ability, preserve, protect and defend the Constitution of the United States."

Section. 2.

The President shall be Commander in Chief of the Army and Navy of the United States, and of the Militia of the several States, when called into the actual Service of the United States; he may require the Opinion, in writing, of the principal Officer in each of the executive Departments, upon any Subject relating to the Duties of their respective Offices, and he shall have Power to grant Reprieves and Pardons for Offences against the United States, except in Cases of Impeachment.

He shall have Power, by and with the Advice and Consent of the Senate, to make Treaties, provided two thirds of the Senators present concur; and he shall nominate, and by and with the Advice and Consent of the Senate, shall appoint Ambassadors, other public Ministers and Consuls, Judges of the supreme Court, and all other Officers of the United States, whose Appointments are not herein otherwise provided for, and which shall be established by Law: but the Congress may by Law vest the Appointment of such inferior Officers, as they think proper, in the President alone, in the Courts of Law, or in the Heads of Departments.

The President shall have Power to fill up all Vacancies that may happen during the Recess of the Senate, by granting Commissions which shall expire at the End of their next Session.

Section. 3.

He shall from time to time give to the Congress Information of the State of the Union, and recommend to their Consideration such Measures as he shall judge necessary and expedient; he may, on extraordinary Occasions, convene both Houses, or either of them, and in Case of Disagreement between them, with Respect to the Time of Adjournment, he may adjourn them to such Time as he shall think proper; he shall receive Ambassadors and other public Ministers; he shall take Care that the Laws be faithfully executed, and shall Commission all the Officers of the United States.

Section. 4.

The President, Vice President and all civil Officers of the United States, shall be removed from Office on Impeachment for, and Conviction of, Treason, Bribery, or other high Crimes and Misdemeanors.

ARTICLE III.

Section. 1.

The judicial Power of the United States, shall be vested in one supreme Court, and in such inferior Courts as the Congress may from time to time ordain and establish. The Judges, both of the supreme and inferior Courts, shall hold their Offices during good Behaviour, and shall, at stated Times, receive for their Services, a Compensation, which shall not be diminished during their Continuance in Office.

Section. 2.

The judicial Power shall extend to all Cases, in Law and Equity, arising under this Constitution, the Laws of the United States, and Treaties made, or which shall be made, under their Authority;—to all Cases affecting Ambassadors, other public Ministers and Consuls;—to all Cases of admiralty and maritime Jurisdiction;—to Controversies to which the United States shall be a Party;—to Controversies between two or more States;— [between a State and Citizens of another State,] (11th)—between Citizens of different States,—between Citizens of the same State claiming Lands under Grants of different States, [and between a State, or the Citizens thereof, and foreign States, Citizens or Subjects.] (11th)

In all Cases affecting Ambassadors, other public Ministers and Consuls, and those in which a State shall be Party, the supreme Court shall have original Jurisdiction. In all the other Cases before mentioned, the supreme Court shall have appellate Jurisdiction, both as to Law and Fact, with such Exceptions, and under such Regulations as the Congress shall make.

The Trial of all Crimes, except in Cases of Impeachment, shall be by Jury; and such Trial shall be held in the State where the said Crimes shall have been committed; but when not committed within any State, the Trial shall be at such Place or Places as the Congress may by Law have directed.

Section. 3.

Treason against the United States, shall consist only in levying War against them, or in adhering to their Enemies, giving them Aid and Comfort. No Person shall be convicted of Treason unless on the Testimony of two Witnesses to the same overt Act, or on Confession in open Court.

The Congress shall have Power to declare the Punishment of Treason, but no Attainder of Treason shall work Corruption of Blood, or Forfeiture except during the Life of the Person attainted.

ARTICLE. IV.

Section. 1.

Full Faith and Credit shall be given in each State to the public Acts, Records, and judicial Proceedings of every other State. And the Congress may by general Laws prescribe the Manner in which such Acts, Records and Proceedings shall be proved, and the Effect thereof.

Section. 2.

The Citizens of each State shall be entitled to all Privileges and Immunities of Citizens in the several States.

A Person charged in any State with Treason, Felony, or other Crime, who shall flee from Justice, and be found in another State, shall on Demand of the executive Authority of the State from which he fled, be delivered up, to be removed to the State having Jurisdiction of the Crime.

[No Person held to Service or Labour in one State, under the Laws thereof, escaping into another, shall, in Consequence of any Law or Regulation therein, be discharged from such Service or Labour, but shall be delivered up on Claim of the Party to whom such Service or Labour may be due.] (13th)

Section. 3.

New States may be admitted by the Congress into this Union; but no new State shall be formed or erected within the Jurisdiction of any other State; nor any State be formed by the Junction of two or more States, or Parts of States, without the Consent of the Legislatures of the States concerned as well as of the Congress.

The Congress shall have Power to dispose of and make all needful Rules and Regulations respecting the Territory or other Property belonging to the United States; and nothing in this Constitution shall be so construed as to Prejudice any Claims of the United States, or of any particular State.

Section. 4.

Zeb Weyrick

The United States shall guarantee to every State in this Union a Republican Form of Government, and shall protect each of them against Invasion; and on Application of the Legislature, or of the Executive (when the Legislature cannot be convened), against domestic Violence.

ARTICLE. V.

The Congress, whenever two thirds of both Houses shall deem it necessary, shall propose Amendments to this Constitution, or, on the Application of the Legislatures of two thirds of the several States, shall call a Convention for proposing Amendments, which, in either Case, shall be valid to all Intents and Purposes, as Part of this Constitution, when ratified by the Legislatures of three fourths of the several States, or by Conventions in three fourths thereof, as the one or the other Mode of Ratification may be proposed by the Congress; Provided that no Amendment which may be made prior to the Year One thousand eight hundred and eight shall in any Manner affect the first and fourth Clauses in the Ninth Section of the first Article; and that no State, without its Consent, shall be deprived of its equal Suffrage in the Senate.

ARTICLE. VI.

All Debts contracted and Engagements entered into, before the Adoption of this Constitution, shall be as valid against the United States under this Constitution, as under the Confederation.

This Constitution, and the Laws of the United States which shall be made in Pursuance thereof; and all Treaties made, or which shall be made, under the Authority of the United States, shall be the supreme Law of the Land; and the Judges in every State shall be bound thereby, any Thing in the Constitution or Laws of any State to the Contrary notwithstanding.

The Senators and Representatives before mentioned, and the Members of the several State Legislatures, and all executive and judicial Officers, both of the United States and of the several States, shall be bound by Oath or Affirmation, to support this Constitution; but no religious Test shall ever be required as a Qualification to any Office or public Trust under the United States.

ARTICLE. VII.

The Ratification of the Conventions of nine States, shall be sufficient for the Establishment of this Constitution between the States so ratifying the Same.

done in Convention by the Unanimous Consent of the States present the Seventeenth Day of September in the Year of our Lord one thousand seven hundred and Eighty seven and of the Independence of

the United States of America the Twelfth In witness whereof We have
hereunto subscribed our Names,

G°. Washington
Presidt and deputy from Virginia

Delaware	Geo: Read
	Gunning Bedford jun
	John Dickinson
	Richard Bassett
	Jaco: Broom
Maryland	James McHenry
	Dan of St Thos. Jenifer
	Danl. Carroll
Virginia	John Blair
	James Madison Jr.
North Carolina	Wm. Blount
	Richd. Dobbs Spaight
	Hu Williamson
South Carolina	J. Rutledge
	Charles Cotesworth Pinckney
	Charles Pinckney
	Pierce Butler
Georgia	William Few
	Abr Baldwin
New Hampshire	John Langdon
	Nicholas Gilman
Massachusetts	Nathaniel Gorham
	Rufus King
Connecticut	Wm. Saml. Johnson
	Roger Sherman
New York	Alexander Hamilton
New Jersey	Wil: Livingston
	David Brearley
	Wm. Paterson
	Jona: Dayton
Pennsylvania	B Franklin
	Thomas Mifflin
	Robt. Morris
	Geo. Clymer
	Thos. FitzSimons
	Jared Ingersoll
	James Wilson
	Gouv Morris

Attest William Jackson Secretary

THE U.S. BILL OF RIGHTS

The Preamble to The Bill of Rights

Congress of the United States begun and held at the City of New-York, on Wednesday the fourth of March, one thousand seven hundred and eighty nine.

THE Conventions of a number of the States, having at the time of their adopting the Constitution, expressed a desire, in order to prevent misconstruction or abuse of its powers, that further declaratory and restrictive clauses should be added: And as extending the ground of public confidence in the Government, will best ensure the beneficent ends of its institution.

RESOLVED by the Senate and House of Representatives of the United States of America, in Congress assembled, two thirds of both Houses concurring, that the following Articles be proposed to the Legislatures of the several States, as amendments to the Constitution of the United States, all, or any of which Articles, when ratified by three fourths of the said Legislatures, to be valid to all intents and purposes, as part of the said Constitution; viz.

ARTICLES in addition to, and Amendment of the Constitution of the United States of America, proposed by Congress, and ratified by the Legislatures of the several States, pursuant to the fifth Article of the original Constitution.

AMENDMENT I

Congress shall make no law respecting an establishment of religion, or prohibiting the free exercise thereof; or abridging the freedom of speech, or of the press; or the right of the people peaceably to assemble, and to petition the Government for a redress of grievances.

AMENDMENT II

A well-regulated Militia, being necessary to the security of a free State, the right of the people to keep and bear Arms, shall not be infringed.

AMENDMENT III

No Soldier shall, in time of peace be quartered in any house, without the consent of the Owner, nor in time of war, but in a manner to be prescribed by law.

AMENDMENT IV

The right of the people to be secure in their persons, houses, papers, and effects, against unreasonable searches and seizures, shall not be violated, and no Warrants shall issue, but upon probable cause, supported by Oath or affirmation, and particularly describing the place to be searched, and the persons or things to be seized.

AMENDMENT V

No person shall be held to answer for a capital, or otherwise infamous crime, unless on a presentment or indictment of a Grand Jury, except in cases arising in the land or naval forces, or in the Militia, when in actual service in time of War or public danger; nor shall any person be subject for the same offence to be twice put in jeopardy of life or limb; nor shall be compelled in any criminal case to be a witness against himself, nor be deprived of life, liberty, or property, without due process of law; nor shall private property be taken for public use, without just compensation.

AMENDMENT VI

In all criminal prosecutions, the accused shall enjoy the right to a speedy and public trial, by an impartial jury of the State and district wherein the crime shall have been committed, which district shall have been previously ascertained by law, and to be informed of the nature and cause of the accusation; to be confronted with the witnesses against him; to have compulsory process for obtaining witnesses in his favor, and to have the Assistance of Counsel for his defence.

AMENDMENT VII

In Suits at common law, where the value in controversy shall exceed twenty dollars, the right of trial by jury shall be preserved, and no fact tried by a jury, shall be otherwise re-examined in any Court of the United States, than according to the rules of the common law.

AMENDMENT VIII

Excessive bail shall not be required, nor excessive fines imposed, nor cruel and unusual punishments inflicted.

AMENDMENT IX

The enumeration in the Constitution, of certain rights, shall not be construed to deny or disparage others retained by the people.

AMENDMENT X

The powers not delegated to the United States by the Constitution, nor prohibited by it to the States, are reserved to the States respectively, or to the people.

To see the other seventeen amendments and as well as explanatory commentary visit

www.heritage.org/constitution

Also visit my website to find other helpful resources as well as read deeper into the resources I used to write this book.

www.daretobeamerican.com

Please report typos and errors to

book@daretobeamerican.com

ABOUT THE AUTHOR

Zeb Weyrick is a part of the young generation that is inheriting the debt, regulations, and the well-meaning yet disastrous policies that have been created in America over the past few decades. He is concerned about his generations future and the opportunities and freedoms that they are currently being tricked into giving away. Zeb is independent and has learned to create his own path, he does not trust the current education system, and because of that designed his own education. He strives to create an alternative to the traditional and corrupted education system and revive the American dream for millions who have not had the opportunities that America is so well known for. Zeb is an entrepreneur and a believer in the opportunities of the free market, he lives in snowy Minnesota and has a passion for motorsports, guns, and politics.

Zeb also has a strong faith in Jesus Christ and believes that he is called to create and renew opportunities for others. He believes that America and the original American way were inspired by God but let down and abandoned by the current church body. He believes that it is his job to point out this fact and encourage those who do follow God to be the biggest fighters for the original American way.

CITATIONS

INTRODUCTION

Page i: "debt up to 19 trillion" "REPORTS." Government. Accessed February 03, 2016.
http://treasurydirect.gov/govt/reports/pd/debttothepenny.htm.

1 WILL YOU DARE?

Page 1: "I hope you make good use of it" Letter from John Adams to Abigail Adams, 26 April 1777 [electronic edition]. Adams Family Papers: An Electronic Archive. Massachusetts Historical Society.
http://www.masshist.org/digitaladams/

Page 3: "Of the people, By the people, For the people" Lincoln, Abraham. "The Gettysburg Address." Accessed February 03, 2016.
http://www.abrahamlincolnonline.org/lincoln/speeches/gettysburg.htm.

Page 4: "Frequent Reference Question: How Many Federal Laws Are There?" LOC.gov. Accessed February 04, 2016.
http://blogs.loc.gov/law/2013/03/frequent-reference-question-how-many-federal-laws-are-there/

2 AMERICAN ROOTS

Page 8: "without a general knowledge among the people" Adams, John. "A Dissertation on the Canon and Feudal Law | Teaching American History." Teaching American History. Accessed February 03, 2016.
http://teachingamericanhistory.org/library/document/a-dissertation-on-the-canon-and-feudal-law/ O "English Bible History: Timeline of How We Got the English Bible." Greatsite.com. Accessed February 04, 2016.
http://www.greatsite.com/timeline-english-bible-history/

Page 9: "Luther's 95 Theses." Bible Study Tools. Accessed March 22, 2016.
http://www.biblestudytools.com/history/creeds-confessions/luther-95-theses.html O "Pilgrim Hall Museum - About the Pilgrims - The Pilgrim Story." Pilgrimhallmuseum.org. Accessed February 04, 2016.
http://www.pilgrimhallmuseum.org/ap_pilgrim_story.htm

Page 11: "Pilgrim Hall Museum - About the Pilgrims - The Mayflower Compact." Pilgrimhallmuseum.org. Accessed February 04, 2016.
http://www.pilgrimhallmuseum.org/ap_mayflower_compact.htm.

3 IDEALS

Page 19: "socialism seeks equality in restraint and servitude" Alexis de Tocqueville 12 September 1848, "Discours prononcé à l'assemblée constituante le 12 Septembre 1848 sur la question du droit au travail", Oeuvres complètes, vol. IX, p. 546 Translation from Hayek, The Road to Serfdom

Page 26: "Net Migration." Worldbank.org. Accessed February 04, 2016.
http://data.worldbank.org/indicator/SM.POP.NETM?order=wbapi_data

_value_2012 wbapi_data_value wbapi_data_value-first ○ "Top 25 Destination Countries for Global Migrants over Time." Migrationpolicy.org. 2013. Accessed February 04, 2016. http://www.migrationpolicy.org/programs/data-hub/charts/top-25-destination-countries-global-migrants-over-time ○ Maule, Christopher J. "Illegal Means Illegal." Immigrationwatchcanada.org. Accessed February 04, 2016. http://www.immigrationwatchcanada.org/2009/08/11/illegal-means-illegal/

4 THE FOUNDING DOCUMENTS

Page 28: "but to overthrow the men who pervert it" Lincoln, Abraham. "Campaign Speech." Speech, Campaign in Kansas and Ohio, September 16-17, 1859. Accessed March 4, 2016. http://www.loc.gov/teachers/classroommaterials/connections/abraham-lincoln-papers/history3.html

Page 29-30: "Writing the Declaration of Independence, 1776." Eye Witness to History. Accessed February 04, 2016. http://www.eyewitnesstohistory.com/jefferson.htm ○ "Thomas Jefferson Biography." Bio.com. Accessed March 07, 2016. http://www.biography.com/people/thomas-jefferson-9353715 ○ "The Declaration of Independence." The Heritage Foundation. Accessed February 04, 2016. http://www.heritage.org/initiatives/first-principles/primary-sources/the-declaration-of-independence

Page 31-32: "James Madison, Father of the U.S. Constitution." Constitution Facts. Accessed February 04, 2016. https://www.constitutionfacts.com/us-constitution-amendments/james-madison/ ○ "Constitutional Convention Begins." History.com. Accessed February 04, 2016. http://www.history.com/this-day-in-history/constitutional-convention-begins ○ "The Constitution." The White House. Accessed February 04, 2016. https://www.whitehouse.gov/1600/constitution

Page 33: "James Madison." Bio.com. Accessed April 14, 2016. http://www.biography.com/people/james-madison-9394965#early-life ○ "Bill of Rights." National Archives and Records Administration. Accessed February 04, 2016. http://www.archives.gov/exhibits/charters/bill_of_rights.html

5 WHY AMERICA IS IMPORTANT

Page 37: "is a plant of rapid growth" "Letter to James Madison." Teaching American History. Accessed February 04, 2016. http://teachingamericanhistory.org/library/document/letter-to-james-madison-12/

Page 38: "Louisiana Purchase." History.com. Accessed February 04, 2016. http://www.history.com/topics/louisiana-purchase

Page 39: "Indian Treaties and the Removal Act of 1830 - 1830–1860 - Milestones - Office of the Historian." Office of the Historian. Accessed February 05, 2016. https://history.state.gov/milestones/1830-1860/indian-treaties ○ "Mexican-American War | Mexico-United States [1846-1848]." Encyclopedia Britannica Online. Accessed February 05, 2016. http://www.britannica.com/event/Mexican-American-War ○

"The Real Histories Directory." Real Histories. Accessed February 05, 2016. http://www.realhistories.org.uk/articles/archive/europe-and-the-slave-trade.html ◯ "Slavery Timeline 1501-1600." Brycchancarey.com. Accessed February 05, 2016 http://www.brycchancarey.com/slavery/chrono3.htm ◯ "CHRONOLOGY-Who Banned Slavery When?" Reuters. 2007. Accessed February 05, 2016. http://www.reuters.com/article/uk-slavery-idUSL1561464920070322

Page 40: "Jefferson's "original Rough Draught" of the Declaration of Independence." LOC.gov. Accessed February 05, 2016. https://www.loc.gov/exhibits/declara/ruffdrft.html ◯ "Slavery Today | Different Types of Human Trafficking - End Slavery Now." End Slavery Now. Accessed February 05, 2016. http://www.endslaverynow.org/learn/slavery-today

Page 44: "Foreign Aid Dashboard." Foreign Aid Dashboard. Accessed February 05, 2016. https://explorer.usaid.gov/aid-dashboard.html#2013 ◯ "Federal Spending by the Numbers, 2013: Government Spending Trends in Graphics, Tables, and Key Points." The Heritage Foundation. Accessed February 05, 2016. http://www.heritage.org/research/reports/2013/08/federal-spending-by-the-numbers-2013 ◯ "Annual Report | Feed My Starving Children." Feed My Starving Children. Accessed February 05, 2016. https://www.fmsc.org/annualreport

Page 45: "Projected GDP Ranking (2015-2020)." Statistics Times. Accessed February 05, 2016. http://statisticstimes.com/economy/projected-world-gdp-ranking.php ◯ Levinson, Marc. U.S. Manufacturing in International Perspective. R42135. Accessed February 5, 2016. https://fas.org/sgp/crs/misc/R42135.pdf ◯ "Capitalism's Triumph." National Review Online. Accessed March 22, 2016. http://www.nationalreview.com/article/358771/capitalisms-triumph-michael-tanner

Page 46: Prager, Dennis. "Why America Is Still the Best Hope." Townhall.com. Accessed February 05, 2016. http://townhall.com/columnists/dennisprager/2012/04/24/why_america_is_still_the_best_hope/page/full

Page 47: "COMMON CORE EXEC REVEALS ANTI-AMERICAN AGENDA: Guns, STDs & Islam." Project Veritas. 2016. Accessed March 22, 2016. http://projectveritas.com/posts/news/common-core-exec-reveals-anti-american-agenda-guns-stds-islam

7 RESPONSABILITY

Page 57: "each individual is accountable for his actions" Republican National Convention, Platform Committee Meeting. By Ronald Reagan. Florida, Miami, July 31, 1968

Page 62-63: O'Reilly, Lara. "Red Bull Will Pay $10 To Customers Disappointed The Drink Didn't Actually Give Them 'Wings'" Business Insider. 2014. Accessed March 17, 2016. http://www.businessinsider.com/red-bull-settles-false-advertising-lawsuit-for-13-million-2014-10 ◯ "HONDA OF AMERICA MANUFACTURING INC v. NORMAN." Findlaw. Accessed March 17, 2016. http://caselaw.findlaw.com/tx-court-of-appeals/1353575.html

8 DO YOUR OWN HOMEWORK

Page 65: "bearing every authority which stood in their way" Thomas Jefferson to Thomas Cooper. February 10, 1814. Accessed February 5, 2016. http://founders.archives.gov/documents/Jefferson/03-07-02-0117

Page 67: "Obama Admin. Knew Millions Could Not Keep Their Health Insurance - NBC News." NBC News. Accessed March 17, 2016. http://www.nbcnews.com/news/other/obama-admin-knew-millions-could-not-keep-their-health-insurance-f8C11484394 O "10 Health Care Benefits Covered in the Health Insurance Marketplace." HealthCare.gov. Accessed March 17, 2016. https://www.healthcare.gov/blog/10-health-care-benefits-covered-in-the-health-insurance-marketplace/

Page 69: "First Committee's Design for America's Great Seal - 1776." Great Seal. Accessed February 05, 2016. http://www.greatseal.com/committees/firstcomm/index.html

Page 70: "Psychology Today." Psychology Today. Accessed March 22, 2016. https://www.psychologytoday.com/blog/psychologist-the-movies/201211/remember-the-titans-can-football-reduce-racism O History.com Staff. "Madame C. J. Walker." History.com. 2009. Accessed March 22, 2016. http://www.history.com/topics/black-history/madame-c-j-walker

Page 71: AJ "12 Of The Highest Earning TV Show Hosts." TheRichest. Accessed February 05, 2016. http://www.therichest.com/expensive-lifestyle/money/12-of-the-highest-earning-tv-show-hosts/?view=all\

Page 72: "Obamacare: Before and After - Discover the Networks." Obamacare: Before and After - Discover the Networks. Accessed March 22, 2016. http://discoverthenetworks.org/viewSubCategory.asp?id=1957#LEGAL CHALLENGESTOOBAMACARE

Page 73: StevenCrowder. "Vox Rebuttal: Gun Control Propaganda Debunked." YouTube. 2016. Accessed March 22, 2016. https://www.youtube.com/watch?v=IULSD8VwXEs

Page 76: "the secrets of statecraft" Churchill, Winston. "Churchill By Himself." Google Books. Accessed February 06, 2016. https://books.google.com/books?id=CAURBAAAQBAJ O Kline, Audrey D. "Gun Control in Nazi Germany." Mises Institute. Accessed February 06, 2016. https://mises.org/library/gun-control-nazi-germany O Levinson, William A. "Articles: The ADL and Gun Control." American Thinker. Accessed February 06, 2016. http://www.americanthinker.com/articles/2015/10/the_adl_and_gun_control.html O Haas, Theodore. "Full Interview with Holocaust Survivor, Theodore Haas." JPFO. Accessed February 06, 2016. http://jpfo.org/filegen-n-z/survive.htm O Jobin, D. L. Guns and Gun Control Exposed: He Guide to Understanding Guns and Gun Control. Bloomington, IN: Authorhouse, 2014 O "Holodomor: The Secret Holocaust in Ukraine." Holodomor: The Secret Holocaust in Ukraine. Accessed March 22, 2016. http://www.thenewamerican.com/culture/history/item/4656-holodomor-the-secret-holocaust-in-ukraine

9 VOTE

Page 79: "that your vote is never lost" Nowlan, Robert A. The American

Presidents, Washington to Tyler: What They Did, What They Said, What Was Said about Them, with Full Source Notes. Jefferson, NC: McFarland &, 2012 ○ File, Thom. Young-Adult Voting: An Analysis of Presidential Elections, 1964–2012. P20-573. U.S. Census Bureau. https://www.census.gov/prod/2014pubs/p20-573.pdf

Page 81: "Yes, Clinton Lied about Her Emails." Washington Examiner. 2016. Accessed February 06, 2016. http://www.washingtonexaminer.com/yes-clinton-lied-about-her-emails/article/2567368 ○ Murdock, Deroy "Hillary Clinton and Obama's Lies on Benghazi - Too Many to Count, but Let's Try." National Review Online. Accessed February 06, 2016. http://www.nationalreview.com/article/426289/hillary-clinton-obama-benghazi-lie ○ Cheney, Kyle "Exclusive: Carson Claimed West Point 'scholarship' but Never Applied." POLITICO. 2015. Accessed February 06, 2016. http://www.politico.com/story/2015/11/ben-carson-west-point-215598

Page 82: Qiu, Linda "Fact-checking Ben Carson's Defense of His West Point Scholarship Story." Politifact. Accessed February 06, 2016. http://www.politifact.com/truth-o-meter/statements/2015/nov/08/ben-carson/carson-defends-west-point-scholarship-story/

Page 87-88: Rector, Robert. "The War on Poverty After 50 Years." The Heritage Foundation. Accessed February 06, 2016. http://www.heritage.org/research/reports/2014/09/the-war-on-poverty-after-50-years

10 DON'T FEED THE SEAGULS

Page 91: "it is the idle man who is the miserable man" Franklin, Benjamin. "Benjamin Franklin Quotes. S. Austin Allibone, Comp. 1880. Prose Quotations from Socrates to Macaulay." Bartleby. Accessed February 06, 2016. http://www.bartleby.com/349/authors/77.html

Page 92: Rector, Robert. "The War on Poverty After 50 Years." The Heritage Foundation. Accessed February 06, 2016. http://www.heritage.org/research/reports/2014/09/the-war-on-poverty-after-50-years ○ Tanner, Michael D., and Charles Hughes. "The Work versus Welfare Trade-Off: 2013." Cato Institute. 2013. Accessed March 10, 2016. http://www.cato.org/publications/white-paper/work-versus-welfare-trade ○ Tanner, Michael. "When Welfare Pays Better than Work." New York Post When Welfare Pays Better Than work Comments. 2013. Accessed February 06, 2016. http://nypost.com/2013/08/19/when-welfare-pays-better-than-work/

Page 96: May, Caroline. "Record 94,610,000 Americans Not in Labor Force - Breitbart." Breitbart News. 2015. Accessed February 06, 2016. http://www.breitbart.com/big-government/2015/10/02/record-94610000-americans-not-labor-force/ ○ Jacobson, Louis. "Ted Cruz Says 92 Million Americans Aren't Working." PolitiFact. Accessed February 06, 2016. http://www.politifact.com/truth-o-meter/statements/2015/feb/10/ted-cruz/ted-cruz-says-92-million-americans-arent-working/

11 AMERICA'S FOUNDING

Page 98: "From John Adams to Massachusetts Militia." Letter from John

Adams. October 11, 1798. Accessed February 6, 2016.
http://founders.archives.gov/documents/Adams/99-02-02-3102

Page 99: Starr, Penny. "Education Expert: Removing Bible, Prayer from Public Schools Has Caused Decline." CNS News. 2014. Accessed February 07, 2016. http://www.cnsnews.com/news/article/penny-starr/education-expert-removing-bible-prayer-public-schools-has-caused-decline

O Smith, Samuel James. "The New-England Primer | Textbook." Encyclopedia Britannica Online. Accessed February 07, 2016. http://www.britannica.com/topic/The-New-England-Primer

Page 103: "25 Violations of Law By President Obama and His Administration." 25 Violations of Law By President Obama and His Administration. Accessed March 22, 2016. http://committeeforjustice.org/content/25-violations-law-president-obama-and-his-administration

Page 107: CAF WORLD GIVING INDEX 2015. Accessed February 7, 2016. https://www.cafonline.org/about-us/publications/2015-publications/world-giving-index-2015

Page 107-108: "Charity Navigator - Your Guide To Intelligent Giving." Charity Navigator. Accessed February 07, 2016. http://www.charitynavigator.org/index.cfm?bay=content.view&cpid=1186#.VvGchKmANBc O http://www.charitynavigator.org/index.cfm?bay=content.view&cpid=42#.VvGdh6mANBd

Page 113: "Countries with the Largest Gross Domestic Product (GDP) 2015 | Statistic." Statista. Accessed February 07, 2016. http://www.statista.com/statistics/268173/countries-with-the-largest-gross-domestic-product-gdp/ O "Countries in the World by Population (2016)." Population by Country (2016). Accessed February 07, 2016. http://www.worldometers.info/world-population/population-by-country/ O "GDP at Market Prices (current US$)." The World Bank. Accessed February 07, 2016. http://data.worldbank.org/indicator/NY.GDP.MKTP.CD?page=6

12 BROKEN AMERICA

Page 119: "More Millennials Living With Family Despite Improved Job Market." Pew Research Center. 2015. Accessed February 08, 2016. http://www.pewsocialtrends.org/2015/07/29/more-millennials-living-with-family-despite-improved-job-market/

Page 120: COHN, D'VERA. "Marriage Rate Declines and Marriage Age Rises." Pew Research Centers Social Demographic Trends Project RSS. 2011. Accessed February 08, 2016. http://www.pewsocialtrends.org/2011/12/14/marriage-rate-declines-and-marriage-age-rises/

Page 127: "Prohibition." History.com. Accessed February 08, 2016. http://www.history.com/topics/prohibition O "AP IMPACT: After 40 Years, $1 Trillion, US War on Drugs Has Failed to Meet Any of Its Goals | Fox News." Fox News. 2010. Accessed February 08, 2016. http://www.foxnews.com/world/2010/05/13/ap-impact-years-trillion-war-drugs-failed-meet-goals.html

13 TURNING POINT

Page 130: "we must live through all time, or die by suicide" Lincoln,

Abraham. "The Perpetuation of Our Political Institutions." Speech,
Young Men's Lyceum, Springfield, Illinois, January 27, 1838. Accessed
February 8, 2016. http://www.whatsoproudlywehail.org/curriculum/the-
meaning-of-america/the-perpetuation-of-our-political-institutions

Page 131: Obama, Barack Hussein. "Obama Campaign Speech." Speech,
October 30, 2008. https://www.youtube.com/watch?v=KrefKCaV8m4

Page 132: Howerton, Jason. "Homeland Security-Funded Study Lists People
'Reverent of Individual Liberty' as 'Extreme Right-Wing' Terrorists." The
Blaze. Accessed April 14, 2016.
http://www.theblaze.com/stories/2012/07/03/homeland-security-
funded-study-lists-people-reverent-of-individual-liberty-as-extreme-right-
wing-terrorists/ ○ CBS News. "DHS' Domestic Terror Warning Angers
GOP." CBSNews. Accessed April 14, 2016.
http://www.cbsnews.com/news/dhs-domestic-terror-warning-angers-
gop/ ○ Sahadi, Jeanne. "U.S. Deficit Now Lowest since 2007."
CNNMoney. Accessed February 08, 2016.
http://money.cnn.com/2015/10/15/news/economy/budget-deficit/

Page 133: "Student Loan Resources: Financial Aid & Loan Debt Management
for Students." Debtorg News. Accessed February 08, 2016.
https://www.debt.org/students/

Page 135: "Transforming Our World: The 2030 Agenda for Sustainable
Development." Sustainable Development Knowledge Platform. Accessed
February 08, 2016.
https://sustainabledevelopment.un.org/post2015/transformingourworld

Page 136-37: Rummel, R. J. Death by Government. New Brunswick, NJ:
Transactions Publishers, 1994.
https://www.hawaii.edu/powerkills/NOTE5.HTM

14 AMERICAN NEEDS YOU

Page 142: "with the blood of patriots and tyrants" Jefferson, Thomas.
"Thomas Jefferson to William Smith." Thomas Jefferson to William
Smith. Accessed February 08, 2016.
https://www.loc.gov/exhibits/jefferson/105.html

Page 144: "nor Liberty to purchase power" Franklin, Benjamin. Poor Richard,
1738. An Almanack for the Year of Christ 1738. Philadelphia: B. Franklin,
1737. Accessed February 8, 2016.
http://founders.archives.gov/documents/Franklin/01-02-02-0035

Page 145: "deserve neither Liberty nor Safty" Franklin, Benjamin. Franklin's
Contributions to the Conference. Proceedings of Conference on February
17: Four Drafts, 1775. Accessed February 8, 2016.
http://founders.archives.gov/documents/Franklin/01-21-02-0269

Zeb Weyrick